Dialectical Behavioral Therapy

The Final Guide to take Control of Borderline Personality Disorders, Anxiety, Addictions. Learn Mindfulness, Interpersonal Effectiveness and Emotion Regulation

Table of Contents

Introduction

What Is Dialectical Behavior Therapy?

At this point, you might be wondering what we need DBT for if there are other treatment options that work so well. Simply, DBT is a type of CBT that offers strategies for managing anxiety that are not included in the regular CBT treatments. Some of the strategies are:

- Mindfulness skills to help you be aware of the present moment, pay attention to your emotions, thoughts and experiences in the here and now.

- Acceptance skills to help you learn self-acceptance, accepting other people, and accepting emotions that you've found hard tolerating or managing.

- Interpersonal skills - assertiveness - to learn how to converse with people in an assertive manner to get your needs met, knowing when and how to ask for what you want and how to decline unwanted requests.

- Emotion regulation skills to teach you how to identify all of your emotions, not only anxiety, and manage them.

Dialectical behavior therapy was initially developed by at the

University of Washington by Dr. Marsha Linehan to help suicidal women, however, Dr. Linehan soon discovered that many of the suicidal women she was treating also had many other problems, particularly BPD, which many of the women met the criteria for. Over time, dialectical behavior therapy has grown to be the most scientifically supported therapy for people dealing with BPD.

If you recollect from chapter 1, BPD and anxiety disorders often go together. Dialectical behavior therapy has been used to treat a lot of people with anxiety disorders; they just happened to have BPD as well. Beyond the fact that many people with BPD also have anxiety disorders, evidence indicates that many dialectical behavior therapy strategies and skills may prove incredibly helpful for a lot of the problems that come with anxiety disorders. For instance, studies have discovered that dialectical behavior therapy can be extremely useful for:

- Anxiety disorders and symptoms

- Trauma

- Depression

- Substance-use problems

- Eating disorders

As a matter of fact, the skills taught in DBT are extremely practical and rooted in such common sense that virtually anyone could benefit by having the littlest knowledge of them.

A Brief History of dialectical behavior therapy

When Dr. Linehan began to develop DBT, people were making use of majorly cognitive or behavioral techniques to help suicidal women, with the idea that if they could change the hopeless thoughts coursing through the women's minds or change their actions e.g. increasing enjoyable activities or getting more social support, their lives would improve and would no longer be suicidal. However, Dr. Linehan discovered that many of the patients she worked with were averse to the fact that the treatment's focus was mainly on the things they had to change.

They felt that they were being blamed for their own problems, like their problems were their own fault. Similar to if you were stranded in a dark, frightening forest, being stalked night and day by animals, and a guide came to tell you that you wouldn't be in that situation if you had thought things through, or you wouldn't be so upset about it if you viewed it from a different angle. Following this, Dr. Linehan realized that she had to seek new ways to let her clients know that they were accepted for who they were, and to help them accept themselves as well, before they could make meaningful changes in their lives. Meaning, you have to stop blaming yourself and accept that you ended up in the forest because you took a wrong turn, before you can really begin working to find your way out.

Dialectical Behavior Therapy In A Nutshell

Dialectical behavior therapy is a fairly involved treatment consisting of different parts. These parts include individual therapy, a therapist consultation team, telephone consultation, and group skills training. Although our main focus is on the skills in this book, knowing about the other aspects of dialectical behavior therapy can be helpful:

- Individual therapy: In dialectical behavior therapy, individual therapy takes the form of a one-hour session each week, during which the therapist makes use of CBT to help you achieve goals that are important to you, reduce behaviors you want to stop, manage problems like depression and anxiety, substance use, eating disorders, or self-harm behaviors if relevant, and improve relationships.

- Telephone consultation: This involves the individual therapist making themselves available to you in between sessions for phone calls when needed or even conversations by e-mail or text messages, to help you handle crisis or emergencies. They also help you learn how to apply new skills in your everyday life, and manage issues arising in your relationship with your therapist.

- <u>Therapist consultation team</u>: This involves a weekly meeting, similar to a support and supervision group of DBT therapists that focuses on how the therapists can achieve optimal effectiveness with their clients, deal with the stress that is associated with being a therapist, and learn how to improve at their jobs.

- <u>DBT skills training</u>: This usually involves two therapists and six to ten clients in a weekly group session, where clients learn practical skills in the areas of mindfulness, emotion regulation, interpersonal effectiveness, and distress tolerance.

The dialectical behavior therapy skills is the major focus of this book, where we will discuss how you can use DBT skills to effectively manage anxiety and its problems while also improving your life in other ways, such as increasing your sense of joy and happiness, achieving goals that are important to you and improving your relationships.

There are four different sets of skills taught in dialectical behavior therapy:

- <u>Mindfulness skills</u>: They help you learn how to pay attention to your thoughts and experiences in the present moment and how to live and be aware of the present moment.

- <u>Emotion regulation skills</u>: These skills teach you to identify and understand your emotions better; lessen your vulnerability to negative emotions like anxiety; and learn strategies to manage, accept, or change your emotions.

- <u>Interpersonal effectiveness skills</u>: They teach you to identify your goals in interpersonal situations and subsequently figure out how to ask for what you want, get your needs met, and decline unwanted requests while also improving your relationships with others.

- <u>Distress tolerance skills</u>: These skills teach you to tolerate and handle overwhelming thoughts, emotions or situations that are hard to change by helping you to weigh your options during a crisis; employ the use of distraction or self-soothing; and self-acceptance, accepting your situation, and your experiences for what they are.

In the following chapter, we will outline a road map to these skills, what constitutes the skills and how they can help you. In subsequent chapters, we will help you discover how to use these skills to manage anxiety-related problems, like:

- PTSD

- GAD, worry, and rumination

- Social and other phobias

- Anxiety, stress, and tension

- Obsessions and compulsive behavior

- Panic disorder and agoraphobia

Before we proceed to the next chapter where we'll cover the skills in detail, here are a few important things to note as you learn how to use dialectical behavior therapy for anxiety problems, in order to help you possess the right or most effective mindset as you begin learning the skills.

Balance Your Efforts to Accept and Change Your Problems

Balance is one of the most important factors in dialectical behavior therapy. In fact, balance is central to the dialectical theory which is the driving force of the treatment. Basically, dialectics means tension between opposing forces, similar to the good versus bad, right versus wrong, negative versus positive charges, cold versus hot, thesis versus antithesis.

In dialectical behavior therapy, the opposing forces are acceptance and change. Acceptance is allowing your thoughts, emotions and circumstances to just be what they are for the moment, without feeling the need to modify, change, escape, or discard them. In contrast, to change means to alter your thoughts, emotions and circumstances.

DBT is dialectical, because it requires us to constantly try to strike an effective balance between acceptance and change. We believe that, to effectively deal with emotional problems, you need to balance acceptance and change. If too much focus is on changing your thoughts, emotions and situations, you can face problems.

So chiefly, dialectics has to do with the idea that in any situation, you can choose to accept what's happening, change what's happening, or some combination of both. The challenging part of this is trying to figure out what you need to accept and what you need to change. This is very similar to the Serenity Prayer used in Alcoholics Anonymous: you need the wisdom to differentiate between what you can change and what you can't, when to accept, and when to change.

In dialectical behavior therapy, maybe even more than is obtainable in other treatments, we spend a lot of time helping people discover ways to balance change and acceptance and find some kind of combination of the two that works best for them.

Let's have a scenario where you are depressed, and you've been spending a lot of time in bed, avoiding phone calls, feeling empty and sad most of the time. You find it difficult to concentrate and you have a lot of negative thoughts about yourself. In this scenario, a synthesis or combination of acceptance and change might be something like:

- Accepting your depressed state, accepting that you feel sad and empty most of the time, and that you have been and are currently inactive.

- Decide to get up slowly and pull yourself out of depression by becoming active, dealing with some of the problems that are contributing to your depressed state, and implement important changes in your life.

Below are a few other examples of this combination, synthesis, or balance of acceptance and change:

- When a relationship is in tatters, you usually have to acknowledge and accept the fact that you have hurt someone and feel the guilt before you can successfully repair the relationship.

- In dealing with OCD, you have to accept that you have obsessive thoughts and also work to alter your repetitive compulsive behaviors.

- The most effective way to change panic symptoms is usually to accept, sit with, and experience your panic symptoms, rather than actively trying to escape or change them.

- At times, the best way to accept and deal with the overwhelming feeling of having too many tasks to do is to change things by dividing your tasks into smaller, more manageable parts.

- If you're afraid of speaking in public, the most effective way to overcome this is to accept the anxiety and fear you experience, after which you should switch the focus of your attention so that you're not paying attention to your own bodily symptoms but more to your audience. Oftentimes, the best way to handle worry is to accept that you're worrying about something, improve your skills at estimating whether something bad will happen, and alter or prevent the things you can.

- If you are struggling with obsessive religious thoughts like if you might offend God if you wore a particular type of shirt, sometimes the best way to break free is to acknowledge that you really don't know what might happen, and then go ahead to wear the shirt anyway.

Do Your Best to Avoid Avoiding

Another way is to start working on lessening the frequency with which you avoid unwanted thoughts, emotions and situations. As discussed in chapter 1, avoiding things too much can be a big problem when it comes to anxiety problems. Dialectical behavior therapy skills in this book will teach you several strategies to help you stop avoiding your thoughts and emotions.

A leading expert in the treatment of anxiety disorders, David Barlow, has opined that one of the most crucial things people with anxiety problems can do is learning to not avoid their emotions. Now, you might be thinking it's not exactly easy to stop avoiding emotions, and it's perfectly understandable because when you regularly experience really uncomfortable feelings, avoidance is a natural response. All things considered, and with some exceptions, many people don't like to feel discomfort. For example, if you are anxious about public speaking or in social situations, you might avoid anxiety by shying away from people and avoiding all avenues to talk in front of people. These strategies are effective in the short term, because they make you feel calmer and less anxious and for this reason, people keep avoiding situations that trigger anxiety. This is known as negative reinforcement: when you keep up a certain behavior because it removes something you don't want.

However, the problem with this is that avoidance just fans the flames of the fear and anxiety. If you never see friends, attend a party or talk in front of people, you never have the chance to learn that the things you were afraid of - humiliation or embarrassment - doesn't usually happen or even if it happens, isn't as bad. So, you continue to live in fear and anxiety. But if you stopped avoiding such anxiety-provoking situations, over time, your brain would learn to stop activating the panic - anxiety-fear button, provided that nothing really bad happened.

Another negative effect of avoidance is that there is often a rebound effect, which is seen when the thoughts you try to avoid are the same ones that seem to keep reoccurring. Some research studies have shown that when you try to avoid or suppress your thoughts, they tend to return with a vengeance. Suppressing or avoiding thoughts and emotions is quite similar to trying to prevent a flood of people from pushing through your front door into your house. If you lose guard at any point, they might just make it through that door, similarly, if you get distracted and stop trying to avoid your thoughts or emotions, they'll come flooding through.

Another option to prevent these people from getting into your house is to bolt the door shut and board up all the windows and entryways in your house. But the problem with this is that you may never be able to leave your own house, and when applied to thoughts and feelings, you can't completely block them out without blocking out most of your life.

Alternatively, if you let the people in through the door one after the other and you carefully look at who is coming in, you might be able to deal with them or at least to face them without so much fear. This is an example of acceptance. Summarily, dialectical behavior therapy is a cognitive behavioral therapy that incorporates several other helpful skills beyond regular dialectical behavior therapy. When learning DBT skills, it is essential to focus on balancing your acceptance of your problems versus how much you want to change them, particularly regarding anxiety problems. Additionally, it is also important to try to lessen your avoidance of thoughts and emotions, and try to cope in other ways that don't involve avoidance. In the following chapters, we will discuss skills that will help you accept and tolerate your thoughts and emotions, and stop avoiding them.

Chapter 1 - DBT Mindfulness and Distress Tolerance Skills

In this section, we will help you gain a good understanding of the DBT skills that will be used to address your anxiety symptoms. Here, we will provide you with a road map to the dialectical behavior therapy skills.

If you recollect, we discussed how avoidance can be one of the things that fuels anxiety problems and disorders, therefore in this chapter, you will be introduced to two sets of dialectical behavior therapy skills that can help you break harmful avoidance patterns. You will also learn to accept, tolerate, and be present at each moment of your life, even in extremely difficult circumstances: mindfulness and distress tolerance skills. This chapter contains a description of what these skills are all about, how they might be helpful, and a couple of practice exercises to help you get started with them. Subsequent chapters will dwell on how each skill can be applied to specific anxiety symptoms.

DBT Mindfulness Skills

With DBT mindfulness skills, you will learn to pay attention to your present thoughts, emotions and experiences. Mindfulness simply entails paying attention to your experiences in the here and now. It is used in numerous types of treatments and has its roots in both Eastern and Western spiritual practices. You are not required to become a Zen master or meditate or sit for long hours on an uncomfortable mat with incense burning in the corner before you can be mindful, all you need to have is a willingness to awaken your mind to happenings around you right here and right now.

Mindfulness Is the Foundation for the Other Skills

A major reason why mindfulness is the first thing we talk about is because it is needed to effectively use any of the other skills discussed in this book. Mindfulness is a fundamental skill that requires you to pay attention to your actions and experiences and by doing this, it helps you put the other skills into action. In the initial stages of learning new skills, you have pay close attention to what you're doing, be mindful and maybe even explain to yourself the steps you're taking towards applying the skills. In this manner, mindfulness can be likened to the foundation of a house; the rest of the DBT skills and strategies are built on top of it.

Most likely because mindfulness is very crucial in DBT, many people have declared that it was the most helpful skill they ever learned. In fact, people often tell us that simply practicing these skills and learning to be present and aware in their daily lives can be life-changing. Furthermore, there are many benefits to your learning mindfulness skills, especially when it comes to anxiety.

Being Mindful in Daily Life

The most effective way to practice mindfulness is to simply pick an everyday activity and do it mindfully, while paying attention to ongoing events, rather than getting distracted by concerns, thoughts, or worries about the past or future. For instance, there so many ways you can take a walk down the street on a beautiful autumn day:

<u>Stuck in your head</u>: Your body could be doing the walk down the street, while you may be thinking about other things such as worrying about a test, working out your finances, or dwelling on things that went wrong in the past or those that might go wrong in the future. Or you could be consumed with anxious or distressing thoughts that pull you away from the present and prevent you from even noticing your surroundings. You can walk down the street in that way

<u>Just getting where you're going</u>: Another way would be to be

solely focused on reaching your destination. Which means walking quickly, looking straight ahead, dodging people as they get in your way, trying to beat lights at crosswalks, avoiding eye contact and random conversations with people on the road, just basically focused on where you are going and how to reach it. Mindfulness expert Dr. Jon Kabat-Zinn would calls this being in "doing" mode. A mode where you're totally focused on accomplishing a target instead of experiencing your life in the present moment.

<u>Mindfully</u>: This is yet another way to walk down the street; awakening your mind to your surroundings, watching the leaves as they drift gently to the sidewalk; the shapes and styles of the buildings you pass, paying attention to the colors in the trees, and the way light reflects off the trees and passing cars; feeling the tender hands of the breeze on your face, what the pavement or trail feels like under your feet etc. This would be more similar to what Dr. Kabat-Zinn calls being in "being" mode. This is when you're fully present in the moment, paying attention to and experiencing the here and now.

As strange as it may sound, the third way of using mindfulness skills or walking sounds pretty simple but is potentially the most difficult of the three. It is usually easier and more natural to be caught up in your thoughts the whole time, not paying attention to what's right in front of you. As a matter of fact, many people spend much of their lives being in their heads. But this third way of walking is the example of how you would walk if you were practicing mindfulness, that'll help you develop better connections with positive and rich present-moment experiences, which is something many people often miss out on when they're in their heads.

The Basics of DBT Mindfulness Skills

There are several types of mindfulness skills in dialectical behavior therapy, but the basic idea is to bring your mind to the present and pay attention to your present experiences. The first step is often to simply pay attention to and be aware of your experiences right now. For instance, when next you drink your favorite warm beverage, coffee, hot tea, cocoa, or something else, observe and pay attention to what it looks like, its color, its aroma, the way it swirls in the cup when you pick it up, the feeling in your mouth, the various tastes that explode on your tongue and so on. Focus your mind right on the present and on the experience of drinking your favorite hot beverage.

Basically, you are required to take a step back in your mind and fully experience the present moment with your senses: sight, hearing, taste, touch, and smell. Closely observe and if your mind wanders, redirect it to what you're focusing on. Don't try to change or escape from the experience you're paying attention to. You can also observe your thoughts beyond your five senses.

Another technique of practicing mindfulness is to label or describe your experiences with words (ibid.). The basic idea is that, while you are drinking your hot beverage, describe to yourself what you notice. For instance, *"the cup feels warm and smooth in my hands"*, *"I see tendrils of steam rising from the cup"* or *"the coffee shows ripples on the surface as I pick up the cup"*, *"It smells "roasty" and smoky"*, *"My mouth feels saturated with warmth."* Make use of words to describe in detail what you see, smell, hear, taste, touch, or think, without including any opinions, judgments, inferences, guesses, or hunches. Don't assume, be concrete and specific. Stick to the facts.

This way of practicing mindfulness is in some ways, the goal of mindfulness in dialectical behavior therapy. This method requires you to throw yourself into whatever you are doing in the present moment. The hot beverage as an example would require you to really immerse yourself in the whole experience of drinking the beverage. Make sure it's the only thing you do in that moment, then throw your entire mind and body into it and make it the most important thing you could possibly do. Do it with vigor and energy.

Similar to other types of DBT mindfulness skills, there are three important things to always remember:

- <u>Do one thing at a time</u>. Ensure you do only one thing in that moment, one thing at a time. As fancy and effective as it may be, avoid multitasking; don't juggle different tasks. Whether the activity is driving, walking, reading a book, eating, washing the dishes, having a conversation, arguing, working, or just waiting in line somewhere, focus your whole mind on the one activity, in the right here and now.

- <u>Avoid judging</u>. Refrain from judging yourself, others, or your experiences. Don't label anything "good," "bad," "right," "wrong," "should," or "should not." If you catch yourself slipping and passing judgments, then redirect your mind to the present or describe only the facts of the situation. Also, don't judge yourself for judging.

- <u>Do what works</u>. You can know what works for you by learning from your experiences and sticking to the things that work. Don't insist on doing things that never work for you just because you want to do or feel like doing them.

Benefits of DBT Mindfulness Skills

A major benefit of mindfulness is that you will fully experience your life as it is right now, instead of being tormented by anxious or distressing thoughts from your past or about the future. In this way, mindfulness can be the solution to some of the distressing thought patterns often experienced by people with anxiety.

We will go on to list some of the other benefits that might accrue to you if you practice mindfulness skills, including benefits specific to anxiety problems and more general ones. Most of the people who have undergone this process confirmed these benefits, and research on mindfulness also supports the idea that many people get at least some of the benefits.

- You learn to be aware of your thoughts, emotions and experiences in the here and now, and also learn to see their true nature.

- It helps you to learn how to take steps back to observe your current situation, notice your thoughts and emotions, and then decide how to deal with them.

- You also learn to step back and experience your emotions instead of avoiding them at all costs. You learn to liberate your mind from worry and obsessive thoughts.

- You live a generally richer and fuller life.

- You acutely enjoy positive experiences.

- You learn to be more present with others.

- You understand your emotions better and have more clarity.

Here's hoping that as we proceed with the mindfulness skills in this workbook, you'll begin to experience many of these benefits in your daily life and in managing anxiety problems.

Get Started with Mindfulness Skills

This is an exercise on mindful observation or how you can use the skill of noticing or paying attention to your experiences in the here and now. Follow these important instructions to get you started:

- Look for a quiet place where you can sit without any distraction for about five to ten minutes.

- Sit in a comfortable position, and sit on a couch, chair, the floor, mats or pillows if you can.

- Begin to pay attention and notice based on these instructions (pay attention to sounds, the sensation of sitting, and the things you see around you).

- If your mind wanders or you need to move, scratch an itch, get up, or stop the exercise for any reason, simply observe these experiences and redirect your mind back to what you were paying attention to. Likewise, if you begin to get swept up in your thoughts, gently turn your mind back to your focus of attention.

Note that mindfulness is simple but not easy; go easy on

yourself if your mind wanders or you find it difficult to do this exercise. That's what minds do; they wander. The whole essence of mindfulness is to bring your mind back to the present whenever it wanders elsewhere. So not to worry, if your mind wanders a thousand times, it means you have a thousand chances to practice than if it wanders only once. Ensure you practice each step of the exercise for a few minutes before you proceed to the next one.

Here are the instructions for mindful observation:

<u>Pay attention to the sounds that you hear</u>. Focus your attention on sounds. Listen attentively, carefully, and with curiosity, listen as if all the sounds you hear were new to you and see what you notice.

<u>Pay attention to the sensations of sitting</u>. Observe what it feels like to be sitting down, notice where the chair or cushion touches your body, and pay attention to any sensations, whether pressure, pain, warmth, hardness, or any other sensation. Anything you notice is perfectly okay; all you need to do is pay attention.

<u>Now shine the spotlight of your attention to the things you see around you</u>. Look down at the floor, and notice what you see there. If you feel any emotional reactions or thoughts to what you see, simply allow these emotions to come and go, then turn

your mind back to what you see. Slowly lift your gaze from the floor, and look at the walls and furniture, if you're in a room with walls and furniture. Pay keen attention to every object you look at and try hard to look at it with curiosity, as if you've never seen it before.

As evident in later chapters, you can apply this skill of simply noticing or observing to other things as well, such as your thoughts, your emotions, your breathing, or practically anything that is happening in the moment.

Try to practice mindfulness skills whenever you can, during a walk, swimming, working, on vacation, worrying, planning, etc. You can always practice mindfulness no matter what you're doing; all you need to do is simply turn your mind to the here and now, and then pay attention.

DBT Distress Tolerance Skills

Distress tolerance skills in dialectical behavior therapy were devised to help people manage emotions, thoughts, and situations that are overwhelming temporarily until things change. People with anxiety problems, are no strangers to overwhelming emotions. Sometimes you just want to curl up and hide somewhere, you want to totally avoid every thoughts or situations that give you anxiety. Although doing this can bring short-term relief, it creates problems in the long run.

There are other techniques to help you deal with stress, overwhelming anxiety and tension, techniques that can help you feel better in the moment and also have long-term benefits. This is where the distress tolerance skills come in, with several benefits for people with anxiety problems and a variety of other emotional problems.

Tolerating Distress

Distress is distressing and people sometimes find it difficult to tolerate distress. All things being equal, many people would likely not choose to feel such intense negative emotions like severe anxiety, anger, shame, sadness, or guilt as often as they do. They'd most likely choose to not have overwhelming or stressful things happen to them, or choose to experience repeated, upsetting, or unwanted thoughts. But unfortunately, these things do happen, and for many, the experiences can be hugely overwhelming that they are lost and don't know their next course of action.

Distress tolerance skills are created to help you particular in those overwhelming moments, when need to do something to deal with an emotional storm until things can change. It's vital to remember that these skills are not necessarily the solution to your problems, but they will help you to tolerate or handle them without worsening it.

In a scenario where you just lost your job or your partner has left you, you are experiencing some unbelievably hurtful feelings, you're anxious and overwhelmed. Here are some different ways that you can react. You might observe that you've done some of these things yourself.

<u>Ruminate and think it to death</u>. You could ask yourself why such things are happening to you. Search your brain thoroughly and think about why you feel the things you do and why these upsetting things are happening to you. Go over it in your mind repeatedly until you've turned over every possible leaf and have arrived at some form of explanation. Worry and think about the implications of the upsetting events happening to you, if there's something wrong with you, and the bad things that might happen in the future. If you're used to this way of coping, you would know that this is one sure-fire path to distress, despair, and agony.

<u>Escape at all costs</u>. Another way to deal with it is to simply escape your feelings and your situations by all means. You could try to avoid and ignore all thoughts about the cause of your anxiety; procrastinate and never do anything about it; you could suppress, clamp down on, or eliminate any emotions that spring up; or you might use alcohol, drugs, binge eating, self-harm or other coping methods to get some relief. If you're someone who has tried any of these, you would probably have noticed that this method of dealing with things never solves

your problems and even creates more problems for you.

<u>Use distress tolerance skills</u>. Conclusively, another way to handle an overwhelming situation is to practice tolerating your thoughts, your emotions, and the circumstances that brought about the feeling itself. For example, you might distract yourself temporarily from upsetting emotions and thoughts by spending time with people, engaging in an activity that captures your attention, or exercising or anything else, until your emotions are calmer and you are able to think effectively and plan better. Also, you could soothe yourself by involving yourself in calming practices like, painting, listening to relaxing music, or taking a warm bath. Additionally, try not to struggle with your emotions or thoughts; instead accept them and let them come and go; keep in mind that your reactions are understandable; and try to accept that you are in an extremely upsetting situation. This third way of coping with overwhelming situations is exactly the whole idea of distress tolerance skills. Doing these things may sound difficult, but rest assured that with practice, it gets less difficult.

The Basics of DBT Distress Tolerance Skills

There are two types of dialectical behavior therapy distress tolerance skills. One involves learning to manage a crisis or overwhelming situation without worsening the situation, until you can effect some changes. These skills are called crisis survival skills. The second type is called reality acceptance skills, which requires that you learn to accept your situation in its present state.

Reality Acceptance Skills

You can tolerate distressful or overwhelming situations by accepting things exactly as they are, and to do this, you have to stop struggling to change your thoughts, emotions, or the present situation. Just allow things to be exactly the way they are.

This may seem kind of strange. In a situation where you are paralyzed with fear about exiting your home, being around other people, or you are tormented by worries, you should not be trying to let go of the struggle to change things. You should not be accepting things the way they are. Why on earth would you want to do that? Well, surprisingly, many people have discovered that accepting things just as they are, at least for the moment, often serves as the only way out of suffering for them. This is in addition to the fact that acceptance is the solution to emotional avoidance, through which many people have found new and life-changing ways to relate to their own experiences.

Acceptance doesn't mean surrendering or giving up, it just means you have to stop the constant struggle to escape from your experiences and just allow them to be what they are. It is possible to accept something and still try to change it. As a matter of fact, to change something in your life successfully, you will likely need to accept it first. For example, you can accept the fact that you are dealing with an anxiety disorder, and doing so might make you less judgmental and feel more at peace with yourself. Alongside reading this book, you can seek therapy or treatment to help yourself.

Furthermore on acceptance, know that you do not need to accept the future. You can accept the past because it has already happened, and frankly there's nothing you can do about it, you can also accept the present situation since it is happening. But, since you don't know what exactly will happen in the future, so then you might need to be wary about accepting it. However, if it helps you to accept things about the future, make sure that the things you choose to accept have a high probability of happening. If not careful, acceptance can easily cause hopelessness about the future when you begin to accept things like I accept that I'll never have a job or never fall in love, or make decent money, or be happy, or be less anxious, etc. Here are a few more important points about acceptance:

- Acceptance is a continuous process. You continually practice but never complete it. Acceptance is not like passing a test or finishing a course; it can be a lifelong practice.

- Acceptance gets less difficult and more effective the more you practice it.

- Acceptance does eliminate your emotions or thoughts; instead it helps you to have them without suffering as much.

- Acceptance doesn't help you to avoid your emotions, thoughts, or life.

Acceptance can seem invalidating. It can be dismissive of the gravity of your problems especially if someone else tells you to do it - "Just accept it!" However don't let that stop you, and don't use acceptance to invalidate your own struggle by yourself. Encourage yourself to stop struggling with reality, and practice letting things be the way they are right now. Note that it doesn't have to remain the same way forever.

Another way acceptance can help you is by teaching you to allow things to be the way they are and do effective or needed things. People often resentfully refuse to accept things as they are or do anything that might help alleviate their situation. Dr. Marsha Linehan labels this willfulness, which involves rejecting reality, refusing to accept things as they are, act as if things were different or as if things were not the way they are, trying to forcefully change things, and refusing to do effective or required things. For instance, your boss makes use of harsh words in an incredibly blunt manner when commenting on your performance, and you and your colleagues see that this will probably not change anytime soon. So you feel hurt and angry every time your boss addresses you in this manner, and you don't want to accept it. In fact, you say to yourself, My boss shouldn't address me this way! This is inappropriate! Then, still feeling angry, you refuse to accept the way your boss talks to you or do anything to help yourself handle the emotional reactions you get when your boss addresses you because you think, it shouldn't be happening in the first place. So you just end up more upset and get the same address in the same aggravating manner the next time, because you haven't changed anything. This is an example of willfulness. Alternatively, if you were practicing acceptance, you could try to accept the fact that your boss has an unfortunate interpersonal style which hurts you, and then work on figuring out what you can do about it. For example, you might make use of an emotion regulation skill to manage your hurt feelings, let your boss' comments roll off your back with the help of mindfulness, or start looking to change jobs, possibly with a boss who has a style more compatible with your needs.

Finally, when you practice acceptance, it is helpful to make a commitment to yourself to embark on the journey. In life, when difficult things happen, it appears as if you have reached a fork in the road, where you have avoidance, worry, denial, rumination, willfulness, and all the things you could do to cause more suffering on one path. And on the other path is acceptance, where you will probably still have upsetting thoughts or emotions but will be able to attain some kind of peace with them. No matter how difficult it is and whenever you need to, try to remind yourself to take this latter path that leads to acceptance.

Crisis Survival Skills

There are a few skills in dialectical behavior therapy to help you get through or overcome a crisis or emotional storm. Self-soothing or relaxation strategies are some of the most basic tools for managing overwhelming distress. One of the things that are most difficult to tolerate about anxiety and other emotions are the physiological experiences that come with them. The increased heart rate; butterflies in the stomach; feelings of muscle tension; feeling flushed, too hot, or too cold etc. As you will learn throughout this book, DBT distress tolerance skills teaches you strategies to physiologically soothe and calm yourself so that your anxiety is a little more manageable. The strategies may not get rid of anxiety or other emotions, but they can render them less intense, which can help you reach the point where you can think and make effective decisions on how to handle your problems.

Distracting yourself is another way to deal with overwhelming distress, even if temporary. This involves doing something that temporarily takes your mind off whatever upsetting situation you are in. We've discussed at length how harmful avoiding your problems, and distraction might sound as just another way to avoid your problems. You're absolutely correct. However, most important here is the fact that research has found distraction to be an effective way of coping with emotional distress. Note that you should use distraction temporarily and not for the long term or to distract yourself your entire life. A very important point to note is that you have to practice distraction mindfully for it to work. You also have to be attentive to whatever activity you are using to distract yourself. If you are thinking about your problems the whole time you're engaging in activities that are meant to distract you, then it won't work.

Any activity that temporarily gets your mind focused on something beyond whatever is bothering you can serve as a distraction. Here are some examples of distraction strategies often used in dialectical behavior therapy:

<u>Getting involved in activities that focus your mind on something other than your problems</u>. E.g., spending time with people, taking a walk, exercising, changing environments, painting or some other hobbies, working or studying and eating (not too much or too little). Make sure these activities are ones that really grab your attention and give your brain some temporary relief from your problems.

<u>Engage in activities that help other people</u> such as charity, animal shelter, helping someone get across the street, offering help to a friend in need etc. Immersing yourself into such helping activities can direct your attention towards themselves and away from your problems while also giving you a sense of self-respect.

<u>You can also use distraction by getting your mind busy</u>. For instance, you might try running through the multiplication table in your mind it subtracting from a number by 7s or 9s until you get to 5 (do this only if you don't have a problem with compulsive counting); solve puzzles; crossword, anagrams, sudoku; play video games or work on a demanding and challenging project.

Benefits of DBT Distress Tolerance Skills

Distress tolerance skills has numerous benefits for people who suffer from anxiety problems, people dealing with other psychological or emotional problems, or even people with no psychological disorders. In fact, practically everyone can potentially benefit from distress tolerance skills. Following are some of the main benefits that might be noticeable if you practice these skills. We hope that you notice these and other benefits as you read this book, especially those that help you with anxiety problems.

- You accept pain in life and suffer less.

- You are more at peace with your problems, even as you try to change them.

- You become tolerable of thoughts and emotions that were once intolerable.

- You stop entangling your mind in distressful thinking patterns like worry and rumination.

- You avoid worsening things.

- You don't have the need to always fix or change things right now.

Get Started with Distress Tolerance Skills

This exercise makes use of the skill of accepting things the way they are. Look for a quiet place where you will not be disturbed, then get into a comfortable sitting position. If your mind drifts during the exercise, just try to guide it gently back to what you're focusing on. Try doing this exercise with your eyes closed.

1. To begin, think of something that you find moderately difficult to accept. To make it easier, think of acceptance as being on a scale from 0 to 100. Choose something roughly in the middle, about 50 or so. Think of that thing

then write down the number that shows how much you accept that particular thing.

2. Afterwards, tense your muscles and fold your arms over your chest. Try hard to get some muscle tension up in your neck, shoulders and arms. Scrunch up your face and furrow your brow to form an irritated or angry expression. Then, tense your facial muscles and think of that thing you're finding it difficult to accept. Focus on it and notice any thoughts or images about it that runs through your mind. Stay in that position for about one to two minutes, then mentally record your level of acceptance from 0 to 100.

3. Next step, relax your body and facial muscles. Open your arms and rest your hands palms facing up on your knees or on the armrests of your seat. Sit in an open posture with legs slightly apart. Try to release all muscle tension in your neck, shoulders, arms or anywhere else in your body. Then, place a very slight smile on your face, making sure the corners of your mouth are only slightly turned up, very similar to the seen on the Buddha, the Mona Lisa or anyone else for that matter who looks serene and at peace.

4. Then, think back to that thing you're finding difficult to accept, Notice any thoughts or images that float through your mind, and allow them roll in and out of your mind. Keep up with this while maintaining your posture and

half-smile. From 0 to 100, note your level of acceptance. Observe if there's any difference in your level of acceptance, ranging from when you started, to when you assumed an angry or tense posture, to when you assumed the more open, relaxed posture with the half-smile. Many people have found that with the more open posture, they are considerably more accepting of the difficult thing. Simply switching your bodily posture or muscle tension can alter your brain activity and neurochemistry and regulate your emotional reactions, making you feel a bit more calm and serene. However, some other people find that this strategy does not do anything for their acceptance level. The trick is to try them and then stick to those that are most effective for you.

At this point in the book, you should have a better understanding of your anxiety problems, a general idea of what dialectical behavior therapy involves, and an introduction to two of the major DBT skills - mindfulness and distress tolerance. Mindfulness and distress tolerance skills have been combined in this chapter because both skills involve you learning to focus on the present moment and accept things as they are, at least for the moment. Whether you're dealing with anxiety or other psychological problems, these skills are fundamental. Here are some suggestions for you as you proceed with these skills:

- Spend a week or thereabouts in regular practice of mindfulness and distress tolerance.

- Set a schedule for practicing the skills on your calendar.

- Endeavor to spend at least five to ten minutes daily practicing mindfulness, acceptance, or any other distress tolerance skill like self-soothing or distraction. The more often you practice, the more these skills will become a habit and less difficult to put into action when you are in need of them.

- When starting, practice these skills to manage mild to moderate problems. Don't practice them for the first time with a tremendously distressing problem that you've been battling for ages, it may not work. Understand that it's a process that will take time and give yourself a break the first few times you try new skills. You will get there.

- Keep in mind the skills that seem to work best for you.

- By now you have a little practice in mindfulness and distress tolerance, therefore in chapter 3 we will begin discussing two other important sets of dialectical behavior therapy skills that you will find highly helpful. They are emotion regulation and interpersonal effectiveness.

Chapter 2 - DBT Emotion Regulation and Interpersonal Effectiveness Skills

If you recollect, in chapter 1, we discussed how helpful it can be to achieve a balance between trying to change yourself and your situation and accepting yourself and your situation. In this second chapter, we will discuss dialectical behavior therapy skills that are helpful for accepting things as they are momentarily and counter avoidance. Here, we slightly balance things out by guiding you through some skills that'll help you change things, in more specific terms, strategies that'll help you change and manage your emotions (emotion regulation skills), and your relationships and interactions (interpersonal effectiveness skills).

DBT Emotion Regulation Skills and Emotions

Emotion regulation skills is an important set of skills taught in dialectical behavior therapy. They can help you enhance the way you manage or regulate your emotions. Studies have defined emotion regulation as the ways people influence their emotional states, and how they experience emotions and express it (Gross 1998). Professionals have observed that the inability to regulate emotion is a common thread across many emotional problems and disorders. People who have anxiety disorders, personality disorders, depression, substance use problems, and "psychotic disorders" e.g schizophrenia, all have at least some form of difficulty with how they manage their emotions. These skills can also be extremely useful for people who don't have any specific emotional disorder. Everybody could use some helpful hints on how to manage our emotions more effectively.

For effective management of your emotions, you have to first be aware of what exactly you're dealing with: what are emotions anyway? Scientists who study emotions define them as a set of reactions in the body and brain in response to events, memories, and thoughts. In a manner of speaking, emotional reactions have different parts and in dialectical behavior therapy, we emphasize the fact that emotions consist of many parts that all work together as one big system, involving your body, your brain, thoughts and actions.

Emotions and Your Brain

The brain is a major part of our emotions such that when we feel an emotion, changes occur in the brain and neurochemistry. For example, when experiencing an emotional reaction, an area in the brain known as amygdala becomes very active. The amygdala is an area in the limbic system involved in motivation, memory, emotions, pleasure, among other things. Think of the amygdala as the emotional engine of the brain that gets revved up when an emotional reaction is triggered.

Another notable area in the brain is the prefrontal cortex. This area is just behind and above your eyes, and is involved in thinking, processing information, decision making, planning, curbing impulses, solving problems, and many other functions. As the amygdala serves as the emotional engine that revs up when you put your foot on the gas, areas of the prefrontal cortex are like the brakes; helping you slow down activity in the amygdala and regulating your emotional state to a baseline or normal level.

The hippocampus - also in the limbic system - is yet another area of your brain. It is involved in learning and memory formation. In emotions, the hippocampus helps you form the memories you need to learn from emotional events.

There are many other areas of your brain that become active when emotions are involved, but these three areas are highlighted because they are particularly involved in emotion regulation. Most times when we talk about emotion regulation, it requires your brain learning from your emotional experiences - courtesy of the hippocampus - or applying the brakes - your prefrontal cortex - on emotional reactions that are not good for you.

For instance, if you were angry with your boss because you hadn't received a raise in a pretty long time. So when you mentioned it to your boss, you raised your voice, which got you reprimanded and embarrassed. In this instance, your amygdala was most likely quite active when you were angry with your boss, while when you raised your voice, your prefrontal cortex was probably trying its best to slow down and limit your emotional reactions to help you think things through, which failed in this case. When your boss reprimanded you and you felt some embarrassment, your amygdala was likely active again, after which your hippocampus possibly kicked in so that your brain remembered that it's not a great idea to raise your voice at your boss.

Emotions and Your Body

Another area of your emotions is the changes that occur in your body when you have an emotion. There are many bodily changes that happen when you experience an emotion such as changes in heart rate, muscle tension, body temperature, other activities that happen in the hormones, sweat glands, tear ducts, and other physical functions. Whenever you feel extremely angry, you may feel an increase in muscle tension, a change in your heart rate by increasing, decreasing, or pounding. You may also notice some changes in your face e.g., a flushing sensation.

Emotions can also cause changes in your facial expressions or posture or in how fast or slow you move. When you feel sad, you may notice a heaviness in your limbs, a slowness to your movements and rate of speech, or a reduction in your tone of voice and change in facial expressions. Alternatively, how does your face look, how do you speak, and how does your entire body feel when you are extremely angry? All the different emotions we feel often involve different bodily sensations, as well as varying facial expressions, and other factors. Usually, we know we are experiencing an emotion in the first place as a result of these changes. In addition, a great way to change an emotion is to alter your bodily movements, facial expression or posture. Studies have discovered that the muscles which move when your facial expression changes - e.g. by smiling - activate a host of changes in your neurochemistry which can then modify how you feel.

Emotions and Your Thoughts

Another component of emotions is the thoughts that run through your mind when you experience certain emotions. Think of these thoughts as passengers along for the ride on the bus of emotions. Unlike your emotions, thoughts are the things you say to yourself in your head or the images you can picture in your mind. For example, "Things are hopeless" is a thought that might accompany a sad feeling or total despair and different thoughts often go with different emotions. Thoughts are what you are saying about a certain situation, yourself, other people or your emotions. We will go on to list some of the types of thinking patterns that might go with different emotional states. Note that although this isn't an exhaustive list, it will help provide you with a sense of some of the thoughts that often accompany certain emotions. Also keep in mind that these are examples and you may have different kinds of thoughts from the ones listed that accompany these emotions for you.

- Some thoughts that accompany anger might include: What a jerk. How dare they do this to me? I can't stand her! Why does he always do this? He had no right to say that! This is awful. This is not how it's supposed to be!

- Thoughts that accompany guilt might include: Why did I do that? I really hurt her. I should never have done that. How can I make up for this? I don't know why I keep doing things like these.

- Thoughts that go along with sadness might include: This is so sad. I can't believe this is happening. What do I do? I'm going to miss this person incredibly.

It is important to note that thoughts can both fuel your emotions and be fueled by your emotions. At times, you become angry only after a bunch of angry thoughts run through your mind, while other times you might discover that you get angry and then the feeling of anger sets you down the path to having some angry thoughts. Or, they might just come all at once in one big rush of anger. Thoughts and emotions have a back-and-forth relationship between them, which means you can change your thoughts by switching your emotions, and you can change your emotions by switching your thoughts. However, this is not to say that the problem is in your head if you experience strong emotions. The conclusion is not that thoughts are the major or singular cause of emotional distress, or that all you are required to do is change your thinking and things will be fine. This is not to say that thoughts don't play a role sometimes, but they are only one part of the picture.

Emotions and Your Actions

Yet another aspect of emotions is your behavior or actions when you feel certain emotions. As a matter of fact, several scientists believe that emotions are meant to help animals take action to promote their own survival. For example, feeling fear as an emotion motivates you to avoid dangerous things such as lions, poisonous snakes, etc. However, the problem is that many of the things human beings are afraid of in recent times such as public speaking, meeting new people, or feeling negative emotions are unlikely to kill us. Regardless, fear still has a great survival value. For instance, if you didn't feel any fear, you might not move fast enough to avoid a truck barreling toward you while you cross the street.

Even though we may be unaware, most of the other emotions are also helpful in many ways. Sadness you feel at the loss of a loved one or something can enable you take the time you need to heal and care for yourself. It can also help you get some help and social support. Anger on its own can motivate you to take action that'll help change harmful situations. For instance, protests across history has brought about huge changes in laws and constitutions around the world. Without the anger people felt that led to these protests, the oppressive laws may not have been repealed and they would still be suffering under the laws.

As you proceed with the discussion about emotion regulation skills in this chapter and in subsequent ones, it's crucial to remember four very important points:

- Different emotions accompany different action tendencies.

- Changing your actions can change your emotions.

- Emotion regulation is concerned with changing your behavior, your actions, and, in certain cases, your thoughts.

- It's almost impossible to change your emotions with the sheer force of your will because if you could, you probably wouldn't need the help of this book.

The Basics of DBT Emotion Regulation Skills

As earlier mentioned, emotion regulation is concerned with the ways in which people affect the kind of emotions they have, when they have the emotions, and how they experience and express them. The dialectical behavior therapy emotion regulation skills enable you manage your emotions in three major ways.

Firstly, skills that enable you identify and understand your emotions. If you are able to understand and identify your emotions, you might discover that they feel less distressing, not so frightening and more manageable.

Next are skills to help you lessen your vulnerability to negative emotions. These skills usually involve enriching your physical and emotional self-care, immersing yourself in positive activities, and engaging in things that help make you feel confident and capable.

Last are skills to enable you change and manage your emotions. Some skills involve learning to retreat from, observe, and be attentive to your emotions without actually escaping from or struggling with them. Some other skills entail learning to engage in actions that are direct opposites of what you actually feel like doing when experiencing an emotion. This book will help you use these skills to manage anxiety and its ensuing problems specifically in later chapters.

Benefits of DBT Emotion Regulation Skills

All humans have to regulate or manage emotions on a daily basis to achieve our goals. If you'd never taken any step to manage your emotions, you probably wouldn't be able to achieve most of the things that you need to. We would be incapable of achieving a lot of things if we allowed emotions to overpower us, so we often have to regulate or manage our emotions so as to deal with people and get through each day.

Ever been in a situation where someone close to you repeatedly did something that annoyed you and you felt irritated but didn't actually recognize your feelings or do anything to manage them? Did you ever resolve that feeling? Like a lot of people, you probably left the irritation to keep building until you eventually exploded and did or said something you regretted. As opposed to this, if you had resolved these feelings when they were less intense by either managing them for yourself or trying to get the person to change, it might have played out differently. Summarily, there are numerous benefits you get when you learn how to manage your emotions effectively. Here are a few, but you should notice others as you go on reading this book.

Getting Started with Emotion Regulation Skills

This is an exercise to help you learn some emotion regulation skills.

Just like the mindfulness skills, find a quiet location where you can be without any distraction for fifteen to twenty minutes. Here, there is just one of the several ways to practice emotion regulation skills, but there are more in later specific chapters.

This exercise is to help you understand and identify your emotions. This is the most crucial and first step in learning how to regulate your emotions. Next, we will discuss the steps that'll set you on the path of understanding three aspects of your emotions: your physical sensations, action or urges, and thoughts. After practicing this skill of simply taking a step back and observing your emotions, you will be better equipped to apply some of the strategies for managing emotions talked about in other chapters.

Physical Sensations, Action Urges, and Thoughts

Ensure you practice this exercise when you feel an emotion at moderate intensity at least, either the emotion is positive or negative.

<u>Physical sensations</u>: Sit and be attentive to your feelings. With the skill of mindful noticing previously mentioned, begin by observing the sensations you experience in your body. Notice any increase or decrease in your heart rate or body temperature? Do you notice any tension or relaxation in your muscles? Any sensations in your belly, head, shoulders, neck, back, or other areas? Pay attention to the particular location you feel the emotion. After observing for a couple of minutes, write down "Physical Sensations," and then note the physical sensations that you just observed on a piece of paper.

<u>Action urges</u>: Then, notice any desires or urges that you have to do something. They are called "action urges." Action urges often accompany emotions because the focus of an emotion is usually to get you to do something. Anger, for example, makes you want to attack or eliminate what is making you angry. Therefore, for this part of the exercise, all you need to do is sit and notice any urges you have to do anything. Do you feel like escaping your emotions or you feel like yelling at someone? Or you may feel like just getting up and running? Do you feel like crawling under the covers and sleeping, hiding, or you just feel like doing nothing? Whatever you feel like, just notice it and then write it down.

Thoughts: Finally, pay attention to the thoughts that are running through your mind. What thoughts or images are in your mind? What are you saying to yourself? Thoughts often come with emotions. In fact, thoughts sometimes trigger emotions, and emotions sometimes trigger thoughts. Just notice the thoughts on your mind. Thoughts often come in the form of words or images, unlike emotions that come in the form of experiences sensed in the body, like muscle tension or other experiences. Just notice whatever thoughts are coursing through your mind regardless of what they are. Simply be attentive to them until you have a clear idea of them and can write it down. This is a great start on DBT emotion regulation skills.

DBT Interpersonal Effectiveness Skills

Another important set of skills taught in dialectical behavior therapy is interpersonal effectiveness (IE) skills. These are skills that help you interact effectively. Typically, the greatest feelings of joy, sadness, disappointment, anxiety and excitement all happen in the course of interpersonal relationships. People who have anxiety problems often have difficulties in their interactions and as a result might stay away from people or even avoid leaving their comfort zones altogether out of fear of encountering people.

Interpersonal problems can worsen anxiety and other emotional problems just like emotional or anxiety problems can worsen interpersonal problems. For instance, people with social anxiety disorder will likely avoid situations where they're required to interact, talk, eat, or any of such activities in front of people. They might also avoid being assertive with people, saying no to things people require from you, asking for what you want etc. The problem with this case is that as you continue to run from these types of situations, it gets incredibly harder to manage in the future, which makes you miss out on opportunities where you can learn how to handle such challenging interpersonal situations.

In summary, the more you avoid, the more you lose chances to learn new skills to overcome interpersonal problems. Additionally, in the event that you had learned these skills before or made use of them previously, you might still find that you need a refresher course because your skills have probably become weaker since you've been avoiding people for so long, just like a muscle that hasn't been used in a long time. For instance, a pilot who hasn't flown in many years would probably need a refresher course on flying before getting into the cockpit again.

Hence, even if you try to stop avoiding interpersonal situations, you might not possess all of the skills you need to navigate your relationships, which may cause you to start avoiding again.

Similar to how dialectical behavior therapy emotion regulation skills help people generally, interpersonal skills can be useful for people who have a variety of difficulties, and also people in general. Anybody could benefit from sharpening their interpersonal skills and improving their interaction skills. In more specific terms, DBT interpersonal effectiveness skills will teach you to be assertive by effectively requesting for your wants from others, declining unwanted requests, balancing your priorities and keeping track of your goals in relationships.

Interpersonal Problems to Work On

People have numerous kinds of interpersonal problems and in this section, we will discuss some of the major kinds of problems that the DBT interpersonal effectiveness skills help alleviate. As you proceed in this section, consider whether you struggle or you've struggled with these particular difficulties.

Difficulty Asking People For Things Or Saying No

Some people find it extremely difficult to ask other people for things they want, whether it's something tangible, such as an object or money, or things like help or support and as a result, they tend to avoid asking altogether. If you happen to be someone who does not ask for the things you want, think about the types of problems that may arise due to this.

If we have a scenario where you cohabit with someone who rarely or never picks up after themselves. The first time they do it, you will feel irritated and frustrated, but you go ahead to clean up after them anyway, with the hope that it doesn't repeat itself. But over time, you find that they keep repeating this behavior, you just continue to feel irritated and frustrated but you never talk about it or ask them to change their behavior. What effect do you think this might have on you? You find that you'll probably develop increasing resentment about the fact that you're the only one doing all the cleaning up. You might also find that you begin to feel irritated with them even at other times and one day, things might just blow up. This is what happens when you don't ask people for things you need or to make changes that are important to you and your wellbeing: the problems pile up and escalate till the relationship turns sour.

In a similar vein, you might be someone who finds it difficult to say no to things and in this case, same problems as previously described can happen. You might discover that you keep saying yes to things you don't even want to do or things that oppose your personal values. This you might cause you to feel like you're being taken advantage of, overwhelmed or resentful, with your self-respect dwindling.

Difficulty Knowing How Strongly Or Intensely To Ask, Or How To Say No

Several people also find it hard to determine how strongly to ask for something or decline a request. At times, you may be too subtle or tentative when asking people for what you want, such that you're not taken serious. On the other hand, you might ask for things in a manner too strong or aggressive. The goal is to know the appropriate manner to ask for things. For instance, if you're in a burning building and someone is blocking your only escape, your best option might be to yell, "Move out of the way!" "Excuse me, could you move?", said in a quiet manner is probably not your most effective line of action. Alternatively, in a situation where you're trying to ask your boss for a raise, addressing your boss in the same manner that you did the person blocking the burning building's escape route will probably be problematic.

If you are someone who asks for things in an intense manner, even in how you say no to things people ask of you in close relationships, you might discover that people tend to burn out. However, if your manner of asking or saying no is very timid and tentative, or you use indirect ways and hints, you may find that your needs don't get met, or might end up frustrated that your needs are never understood.

In relationships, it is crucial that you know how to aggressively request or say no to requests. The goal is to be assertive in an appropriate manner instead of being either too timid or too aggressive.

The Basics of DBT Interpersonal Effectiveness Skills

The IE skills in dialectical behavior therapy help you learn how to ask for things you want or say no to requests effectively, and how to navigate your interactions with other people in a way consistent with your values and goals.

Here are some major things you're taught in IE skills:

The first is, you are taught to identify your goals in terms of an interaction. Then how to ask for things, say no to requests or assert yourself appropriately and effectively. Third, is teaching you how to strongly or aggressively say no, or express your opinion.

Identifying Your Goals And Needs

In your interaction with others, it can be extremely helpful to know the goals and needs you hope to derive from the interaction. If not, you could lose sight of what you want from the relationship, or you might not do the things that'll help achieve the goals. In DBT interpersonal effectiveness skills, goals are discussed in three different ways: what you hope to get out of the situation, how you want to affect your relationship or what the other person feels about you, and how you personally want to feel about yourself during and after the interaction. All these goals are very important. Let's have a scenario where you want your boss to give you a raise, but you might lose your job instead if you don't have a good relationship with your boss. So, before asking for a raise, you should consider how you want your boss to feel about you and the relationship. It's understandable that you really want a raise, but if you have to beg and grovel and do all sorts to get it, in the end, you might feel bad about yourself or lose your self-worth. This is why it's important that you think about how you want to feel about yourself during and after the interaction with your boss.

When starting every interpersonal interaction, it is usually helpful to consider what you want to get from the situation in every one of these areas: clarify your goals. Your goals in all three areas are all important, but taking some time to think about which of the aforementioned goals are the most important will help determine your approach.

Asking, Stating An Opinion, Or Saying No

In DBT interpersonal effectiveness skills, you are also taught many primary steps to ensure your opinion is effectively stated, asking for something, or saying no to something:

1. Ensuring that the other person understands what the issue is by explaining the situation clearly and objectively to them.

2. Use statements with "I feel" and "I think" to let the person know how you feel about the situation.

3. Explicitly state your needs and wants from the situation.

4. Ensure to clarify upfront about how this will benefit the other person.

5. Identify ahead of time any compromises you might be open to make to achieve your needs.

6. Additionally, it is vital that you say all of this in a way that fits your relationship goals, and in a manner that doesn't make you feel bad about yourself or make you lose your values.

Say for instance, we have a situation where it's your partner's job to do the dishes, and you repeatedly come home from a long, hectic day of work to find the dishes undone. Outlined is an example of how you might use these skills to communicate to your partner what you need regarding the dishes:

1. "I have observed over time that the dishes are usually not done when I come home from work on Thursdays evening" (here you're explaining the situation).

2. "And it is overwhelming when I have to clean up the kitchen after getting home late" (you're letting them know how you feel about the situation).

3. "Please take some time to clear the dishes after dinner" (you're stating your needs and asking for what you want).

4. "I would be much more less stressed out if you could do this for me." (clarifying how this will be of benefit to the other person).

5. "And I think I could take some time out to clean up on Tuesdays in return" (you're stating a compromise you'd be willing to make ahead of time).

Here are a few tips on communicating in this way. First, you must speak in a manner that will make them willing to listen to you and that they can understand, which means making sure you don't speak too bluntly or abruptly, you don't talk for too long, avoid inflammatory language or passing judgments on yourself or the other party and being concise and straightforward. Secondly, when describing how you feel, use words of emotion like "hurt," "anger," "sadness," "disappointment," "irritation," and "annoyance." Use words that are adequate to the intensity of the situation. For instance, in the previous scenario, you might describe frustration instead of rage. If you can do so without invalidating your own feelings, use softer emotions like sadness, hurt, and disappointment more often than you use harder ones such as anger, frustration, and annoyance. If you express softer emotions, people will probably empathize more with you than if you use harder ones. You can also try expressing your thoughts in an objective way, without using judgments; e.g. "I'm overwhelmed when I get home late in the evening and have to clean the kitchen."

Third, you have to stay focused on what you want and not get distracted due to the fact that it's extremely easy to lose sight of your goal or your reason for starting the conversation in the first place in an interpersonal interaction. It's quite like driving down a freeway toward your destination but taking an inadvertent exit to the middle of nowhere. Similarly, your partner could say things like, "Well, you never do the laundry either, so why are you always talking about the dishes?" The skill helps you to stay focused and calmly reply with something like, "I know what you're saying, but we're talking about the dishes now, maybe we can talk about the laundry later."

Fourth, try to use the interaction as a means of enhancing your relationship. Think of ways to ask for what you want without making the other person feel bad about themselves for giving it to you. You can do this by using a kinder, softer approach and by showing that you're interested and understand what the other person has to say. You can try to use humor or a lighter, gentler approach when you make a request from someone or decline someone's request. You might say, "I understand that you're upset that I haven't done the laundry. I know that you work hard too, and it's annoying when I don't help out sometimes. That's the same way I feel about those dishes."

Benefits of DBT Interpersonal Effectiveness Skills

Interpersonal effectiveness skills can help you enhance your interactions, manage and resolve conflict, while meeting your needs in such a way that you're empowered and you get a confidence boost in your ability to deal with people. If you find that by learning some new skills, you have better experiences with people, you might feel better about your life, improve your social support, and even have more fulfilling and meaningful relationships. All these advantages can help you to maintain the progress you've achieved in managing your anxiety-related problems. Following are some additional benefits of IE skills that are tailored a bit more to anxiety problems:

- Some people who have anxiety disorders feel disconnected from other people. IE skills can help you connect with people and be able to communicate your needs.

- People who have anxiety disorders may not have a lot of social support, so IE can help establish new relationships.

- Some people with anxiety disorders tend to avoid conflict, which may result in their needs not being met, and ultimately causing them to feel worse about themselves. IE can help with this.

Steps for Getting Your Needs Met in Interpersonal Interactions

This is an exercise to help you get started with some IE skills. First, think about a need that you want someone to meet. You might want someone's help or support, or you might want them to change a behavior - maybe doing laundry more often. Make sure it's a situation that is only mildly to moderately difficult. Nothing too hard. Best for you to start with less-challenging situations when you start learning new skills, more like a gradual process. I'm sure you wouldn't be so quick to jump in the ocean if your swimming skills are tentative.

1. Clarify your goals for every interaction.

2. Develop a script for stating your needs and describing your wants.

3. Practice this script as many times as you need until you are comfortable with it. Stand in front of a mirror and practice or practice with a close friend or family. In addition to words, concentrate on your nonverbal behaviors such as your tone of voice, facial expressions.

4. When you feel adequately prepared, approach the person in question and apply what you've practiced. Ask for what you want. Note that this skill becomes easier with more practice. The more you practice, the more comfortable you get, which will make it more likely to get some of your needs met.

Try this and see how it plays out, but do not feel defeated or demoralized if you don't achieve what you want from the situation. Ultimately, you can only do your best, and your best will not always mean that things will work out exactly how you would like them to. Keep in mind that even the most effective people in interpersonal skills don't always get what they want out of the situation. Regardless of how the situation turns out, you can take comfort in the fact that you were as skillful as possible and did what you needed to do. Knowing that can be helpful.

At this point, you should have a better understanding of what anxiety is and what it entails, what dialectical behavior therapy is and how it might help you manage anxiety. In this book, a foundation has been laid in chapters 1 through 3. And the remaining chapters build on that foundation. Proceeding, you will learn ways of applying these dialectical behavior therapy skills in ways specific to the types of anxiety disorders that you have and hopefully at the end, you will have developed a strong set of skills to help you through your anxiety.

Chapter 3 - DBT And Stress

Stress often accompanies anxiety and fear. In fact, they go alongside each other so often that many people use the terms "stress" and "anxiety" interchangeably. However, as closely related as they are, stress and anxiety are not the same thing. There are some important differences that you should be aware.

What Is Stress?

All humans experience anxiety, as well as stress. It is unavoidable. So what is stress, and how does it differ from anxiety? Stress is a much broader term than "anxiety," and refers to your body's response when faced with a circumstance that prompts you to act, change, or adjust to your environment. As explained in chapter 1, anxiety and fear serve important purposes. Through them, the body tells us that we may be in a dangerous situation. Likewise, stress also serves a very important function. Stress basically tells you when your body's resources are being taxed or used up.

Imagine your body as a giant computer. Of course, computers are becoming faster and faster every single day, but ultimately, even the most complex and advanced computer is still subject to only a limited amount of processing power. So, running one small program on the computer will use up a little of the computer's processing capability. This means that the computer now has a reduced processing power for other programs; but, if it's just one small program running, it may not affect the computer's performance all that much.

Now, imagine that you start running several programs on your computer. At a point, you will begin to see a decline in the performance of your computer. Which means, the more programs you run on your computer, the slower it becomes in managing each program. In extreme cases, if you're running so many programs running all at once for an extended period of time, it could tax the computer so much that it crashes.

This is the same way our bodies work. The human body has a limited amount of resources to deal with the situations it encounters. Simply, our bodies have only so much mental or physical energy at its disposal at any given time. The higher the amount of situations or activities that we encounter that exhausts these resources, the more depleted, tense we feel and the less effective we become in handling these situations. Additionally, the longer we remain in these situations or engage in these draining activities, the more depleted our resources get and as a result, it may become even more difficult for us to manage our emotions or be more reactive. Our emotions may even seem more uncontrollable and our concentration may also suffer. We may face sleeping problems, and our chances of becoming physically ill may even increase. When many people think about stress, they think it can only be due to an unpleasant or negative situation like losing their job or dealing with an illness, they don't always realize that stress can result from both pleasant and unpleasant situations. As a matter of fact, even the word "stressful" has come to have negative or unpleasant connotations. Pleasant events or situations that bring about positive emotions, however, can also lead to stress. For instance, having a baby or planning a wedding, or getting promoted can also be stressful events. Regardless of the fact that they're positive situations that bring you benefits, they can also be a source of stress. It is important that you know the types of events that cause stress for you. Once you're aware of these situations, you can be better prepared to cope with the stress that come with it.

Stress in Anxiety Disorders

Though stress isn't actually a specific symptom of any one type of anxiety disorder, the one exception to this may be generalized anxiety disorder (GAD). Before someone can be diagnosed with GAD, they must have experienced a variety of physical symptoms related to stress for more days than not in the past six months, coupled with other symptoms, like uncontrollable and excessive worry. Some stress-related symptoms of GAD are tiredness, muscle tension, difficulty sleeping, and concentration problems.

Although stress is not mentioned as a specific symptom of other anxiety disorders, stress comes with all anxiety disorders. Someone with panic disorder may have some of the physical symptoms of stress, like muscle tension. People who have PTSD may feel high levels of stress due to the fact that they're constantly being on guard. With social anxiety disorder, they may find social interactions extremely stressful. Generally, anxiety disorder symptoms can be very difficult to deal with and can also tremendously impact a person's life, which often causes a great deal of stress, depleting some of your resources to cope with other stressful life experiences.

Managing Stress with DBT Skills

Fortunately, several dialectical behavior therapy skills can help lower your vulnerability to stress, while also helping to manage some of the consequences of stress. Before going on to discuss specific dialectical behavior therapy skills, the first step is to identify where exactly you feel stress and tension in your body, because physical or bodily experiences are usually the first warning signals that you are under stress, the signs that you need to pay attention to.

Think back to times when you experienced at least a moderate amount of stress in your life and try to remember where you felt the stress in your body. Below are some common locations where people experience stress in their bodies.

Using Self- Care to Reduce Your Vulnerability to Stress

As earlier mentioned, our ability to handle stress depends largely on the mental and physical resources we have at our disposal. Taking good care of yourself can increase your available resources, therefore lowering your vulnerability to stress. This is so important that an entire set of dialectical behavior therapy skills is devoted to taking care of your body to enable you have more resources available for when you need to deal with all of the demands and stressors in our lives.

There are a number of things you can do to ensure adequate care for your body.

Maintain Balanced Eating

Feeding your body and maintaining healthy eating habits is one of the ways to ensure you store up on as many resources as possible to help you cope with stress when you need it. Your body is dependent on nutrients to live and function adequately, so maintaining a healthy diet will give you the needed fuel for your body. Just like your car can't function well and malfunctions when it is running on fumes, your body works the same way. You can't function optimally without a full tank of gas, so provide yourself with the fuel you need throughout the day.

Healthy eating actually comprises of two parts. Firstly, you need to eat regularly throughout the day. Space out meals and snacks to "fuel up" throughout the day and try to keep your blood glucose levels as balanced as possible. Some studies have shown that reductions in blood glucose can deplete your available resources, which will make it more difficult for you to manage stress and avoid harmful coping techniques like drinking, doing drugs, smoking, and overeating. Maintaining your fuel tank at a steady level will help you deal with stress better.

Secondly, eating healthy foods is good for you. If you eat only junk food and processed sugars, you'll most likely not have as many resources available to manage stress. To prevent this, eat plenty of fruits, vegetables, proteins and whole grains. They're the premium fuels that will help your body function at full capacity. Of course, there's nothing wrong with indulging occasionally, but for the long term, it's best to have a diet that's consistently healthy and balanced. If you're uncertain of what to eat or how to maintain a healthy diet, you should talk with your general physician or a nutritionist.

Maintain Balanced Sleep

Sleep is one more source of fuel for your body, without which your body doesn't run as well and alongside needing proper nutrients to function properly, your body also needs enough sleep. Lack of sleep or not getting enough sleep will leave your physical resources greatly depleted, which in turn diminishes your body's ability to manage stress. Simply, when you sleep, your body restores its resources and accumulates the mental and physical energy you need for the day. Hence, not getting the full amount of sleep your body requires each night will make your body unable to fully restore your resources, which leaves you with fewer resources available to draw from during the day. Ultimately, you will have fewer resources for managing stress.

You will have noticed that not getting enough sleep leaves you on edge, more prone to getting irritated over the smallest things. This is most likely due to the fact that you don't have the same level of resources available for managing stress as is normal after a full night's sleep, thus, you couldn't handle it well. For this reason, getting a full night's sleep every night is extremely important. Some people find it difficult to get enough sleep every night due to a lot of reasons. An effective way to deal with this is to maintain a regular sleep schedule. Go to bed at approximately the same time every night and wake up at about the same time every morning. Remember that regular sleep equals more resources for managing stress.

Of course this is not always easy to do as many people with anxiety disorders usually find it hard to sleep, as they experience periodic bouts of insomnia, waking early with worries. A technique that can help you deal with these problems is known as sleep hygiene. Sleep hygiene is a set of strategies that you can use to improve the quality of your sleep. The first step in sleep hygiene is to clear out your sleep area by removing clutter from your bedroom and ensure it's a great environment for sleeping. After this, try identifying and changing some of the factors that might be causing your inability to sleep well. Some of these factors might include but are not limited to drinking caffeine, afternoon naps, exercising, watching interesting Tv shows, taking alcohol or drugs too close to your bedtime, or eating a large dinner. Try to change any of these behaviors that may be harming you so as to optimize your sleep. Third, maximize your sleep efficiency.

What is sleep efficiency? This is the proportion of sleep to the amount of time spent in bed. Which means if you are in bed for eight hours but only sleep for six hours, your sleep efficiency is 75 percent. Generally, the main idea is to make sure the number is as close as possible to 100 percent by avoiding engaging in activities beyond sleep in bed. Activities like checking e-mails, watching Tv, working or having important discussions should not be done in bed because you want your brain to connect bed and sleep, not bed and staying awake.

Get Regular Exercise

Regular exercise is another way to reduce your vulnerability to stress. Regular exercise can indeed make your body stronger and build up your physical resources over time. And this translates to you having more resources available for managing stress. Now, regular exercise doesn't mean that you have to work out five days a week at a gym but if you can, then by all means go ahead. However, it's not necessary that you see the physical benefits of exercise before it achieves its purpose. All you really need is to do some sort of moderate physical activity at least thirty minutes a day for five days a week. Note that it doesn't have to be running or jogging or even using exercise equipment. It could be something as simple as gardening, walking, vacuuming, walking up any staircase you can, basically anything else that increases your heart rate. Just make sure you do something that's moderately active for about thirty minutes at least. As earlier mentioned, being busy and having a lot to do can lead to stress and this is the same reason why it can be difficult to maintain a regular exercise program.

Be kind to yourself and get your exercise anywhere and anyhow you can. Going to the store? Make sure you park as far away as possible so that you can walk a bit. If your workplace is in a multistory building, avoid the elevator and take the stairs. While cleaning your house, make sure the cleaning is as physical as possible by moving the vacuum rigorously and really putting energy into scrubbing the floors or any such activities. Lastly, riding your bike to work is a great way to include exercise into your regular routine.

Take Care Of Any Illnesses You Have

Physical illnesses can also use up your body's store of resources, which you need to deal with daily stressors. Therefore, taking care of any illness is a great way to strengthen your resources to get you in top shape for when you need to deal with a stressful situation. Consult your doctor for any illnesses and take appropriate medications. Also, drink lots of liquids and get extra sleep. Call in sick and take a day off work or reduce your exercise routine till you feel better. Just do everything you can to restore your physical health. You don't want to be sick while also dealing with stress. You can manage stress better when you're healthy.

Limit Alcohol And Avoid Drugs

Also note that too much alcohol can use up a lot of your body's physical resources and generally take a toll on you. Similarly, alcohol or mood-altering drugs can tax your emotional resources. So, avoid using drugs and restrict your alcohol intake in order to lower your vulnerability to stress, while also ensuring that your body functions at the optimal level.

Increase Your Self-Efficacy By Doing Things That Make You Feel Capable

Stress can wear on you psychologically as well as physically. That's why you notice that when you feel positive and good about yourself, you are better disposed to handling stress and you don't get easily destabilized by stressful situations like you do when you feel terrible about yourself or feel less capable. This is why feeling stronger and more psychologically capable is how you can effectively manage stress. So, a simple way of making yourself less vulnerable to stress is to do one thing that makes you feel capable and in control of your life each day. Doesn't matter what it is, just do anything that makes you feel in control.

Use Self-Soothing Techniques to Ease Your Mind and Body

Caring for your body and soothing yourself physically throughout the day is quite similar to those skills previously described that help to reduce your vulnerability to stress. You can use these self-soothing skills in dialectical behavior therapy to stave off the negative effects of stress, thereby increasing your ability to manage the stress you face. The skills can help replenish your resources throughout the day and continue to add to them so that when you unexpectedly encounter stress, you are better equipped to handle it. These skills help care for and soothe your body by introducing comforting sensations to all of your five senses. Below are some of the sensations that people find most soothing and comforting.

<u>Touch</u>: initiates sensations that soothe your body and feel good on your skin. Sit in a hot tub or sauna. Have a warm bubble bath. Get a massage. Relax in the sun, concentrating on the warmth on your skin. Play with your pet, focusing on how the pet's fur feels against your skin. Hug a friend or loved one. Wear clothing with soft, soothing textures, such as a warm sweater, a soft flannel shirt, a silk top, a soft cotton sweatshirt etc. Wrap yourself in a warm, fluffy blanket and sit in front of a fire. Focus on the warmth you feel.

<u>Taste</u>: Sip a cup of hot tea or cocoa or any kind of hot drink. When it's hot, take a cold drink, or eat an ice cream bar. Eat your favorite comfort food, e.g. cheese sandwich, mac and cheese, sushi, mashed potatoes, freshly baked bread. Eat a fresh fruit. Eat dark chocolate as it helps to release "feel-good" chemicals.

<u>Smell</u>: Go to a flower shop and smell the flowers even if you have to pretend to buy. Light scented candles and burn incense. Breathe in the aroma of lavender or vanilla. Step outside and

inhale fresh air. Bake cookies or fresh bread, and breathe in the aroma. Brew some coffee and smell it.

<u>Sight</u>: Look at pictures that soothe or relax you, such as pictures of the sunset, a beach, or a beautiful mountain. Look at pictures of family and friends or one of your favorite vacation spots. If you can, go to the beach and watch the waves. Watch your children play or sleep. Watch the clouds and the sunset. Go to a playground and watch children play.

<u>Hearing</u>: Listen to music that relaxes you. Listen to children playing. Listen to birds sing. Take a walk in the park and listen to the sounds of nature. Go to the beach and listen to the sound of waves crashing on the shore.

Using Mindfulness Skills to Deal with Distraction and Poor Concentration

Stress is often very distracting and when people are under a lot of stress, they discover that they are finding it difficult to focus on anything else. Does stress affect you in this way? When under stress, do you find it hard to think about anything else? Ever notice that you spend a lot of time thinking about the causes of your stress and the effect it has on you? If stress affects you in this way, you may find that it hinders you from accomplishing other things in your life, which can in turn complicate things for you by making you feel unproductive. It may even divert your attention from positive things in your life to more stressful things.

Fortunately, dialectical behavior therapy has a skill that can effectively redirect your attention to more positive things, thereby managing this particular symptom of stress. Because the DBT mindfulness skill focuses attention on one thing at a time, it can be used to help redirect your focus whatever you are doing presently. This ensures that your attention is directed to the task at hand when you're distracted by stress. As earlier mentioned, this skill is focused on doing one thing at a time and letting go of distractions. So, if you are listening to music, listen. If you are writing, write. Whatever you are doing that's comforting or self-soothing, concentrate on doing just that. When people are stressed, they believe that their best option is to multitask and work on as many things as they can at once. They do this because they think it will help them to achieve more, and consequently, feel less stressed. This belief is simply false. As opposed to dividing your attention among many things, shunning distractions and focusing all of your attention on just one thing at a time will help manage your stress much more than multitasking can.

Therefore, when next you find that you're getting distracted by whatever your stressors are, take a deep breath and bring your attention back to whatever thing you were presently doing. Concentrate all of your attention on only that one thing and throw yourself into that activity. Notice if your stress distracts you, and then return your mind to the present activity. Repeat this as many times as you need to, and continue to refocus your attention whenever you need to. Remember that the mind gets distracted and so the goal of mindfulness is to notice when you get distracted and then repeatedly refocus your attention where needed.

This skill can also help you to stay strong under stress generally. Dr. Marsha Linehan opined that "When you just do one thing in the moment, you never really get overwhelmed". Ever noticed that your actual stressors are not the things you are doing in that moment, but a feeling of doom or a bunch of worries about the things you need to do in the future? Although, the present moment can sometimes be fairly stressful in itself, if you are focused on the things you're doing presently, instead of the numerous things you need to do at some point in the future, you will feel much lighter and not like you're carrying around the weight of the world. Stick to whatever task you are working on. When walking from one place to another, simply focus on the act of walking itself. Practice this skill whenever you find that all the demands or stressors in your life is overwhelming you, and see if it's effective.

Using DBT Skills to Deal with Emotional Reactivity and Stop Unwanted Behavior

You know all those times that you noticed that you are more likely to lose your cool or easily break down into tears when you are stressed out? It makes absolutely sense because when your resources are depleted due to excessive stress, you are less likely to manage your emotions effectively. Sometimes, you will feel much more emotionally reactive or than others. When you are under a tremendous amount of stress, you're most likely to be emotionally reactive, and you may be unable to control how emotional you are, but you can control your behavior. There are a couple of dialectical behavior therapy skills that focus on helping to control your behaviors when faced with intense emotions. The mindfulness skill of noticing your experiences and the distress tolerance skill of focusing on the consequences of your behaviors before you act are two skills that we believe can be most effective in this area. Here are some steps you can take when it feels like you're at the end of your rope and almost ready to lose control.

- Stop what you are doing. Sit in a comfortable, alert position in a place without distractions, and don't move a muscle.
- Take a step back and observe your experience. Make use of the mindfulness skill of noticing your experience to take a step back in your mind and observe your feelings.

- Notice whatever emotion you experience and where exactly you feel it in your body.

- Scan your body with the spotlight of your attention and figure out where you are holding tension, the sensations you're feeling, your heart rate and body temperature. It's okay for your mind to wander (that's what minds do) simply return your attention to your body. Don't try to avoid any of your bodily sensations or try to escape them. For now, just notice them.

- Notice any urges to act that you have, If you feel angry, frustrated, irritated, or maybe you just feel the urge to lash out at someone. Do you feel sadness, despair, shame, or you just want to run and curl up in your bed? Whatever your feelings may be, just simply notice them. Notice what you feel like doing, the urge or desire to act, and allow it to come and go. Just take a step back and pay attention to it for a little while. Don't try to escape it or try to keep it around you. Visualize yourself riding this urge like a wave on the ocean.

- Consider the consequences of your actions. When stressed out, a great way to steer yourself onto a more effective course is to consider the results of acting on an impulse and doing what you feel like doing. When you're under stress, the immediate positive consequences of actions like throwing things, yelling, drinking, using drugs, etc. are likely to seem pretty fulfilling to you.

Hence, you need to focus your brain on the negative consequences of these behaviors. To achieve this, make a list of all the consequences of both positive and negative behaviors, short term and long term ones.

Urge Surfing: A Mindfulness Skill to Cope with Urges

Look for a quiet place where you will have little or no distractions and sit in a comfortable position. Get a piece of paper and write down how strong your urge is on a scale from 0-10. 0 being no urge at all and 10 being the strongest urge you have ever had. Next, write down how much you think you can handle your urge, on a scale from 0-10. 0 being you can't take it for one more second and 10 being you could handle it for ten hours straight if you had to. Picture yourself in a warm, tropical place standing on a surfboard on the ocean. The white, sandy shore is in front of you, a slight breeze blows the salt of the ocean to your nostrils. The sun feels warm on your back with fluffy, white clouds overhead. Fully immerse your mind to this scene.

Now, imagine that the wave you're about to catch is your action urge. The wave gets higher as your urge rises and becomes stronger, but you stay right on top of it. Imagine yourself as an excellent surfer who can ride any wave that comes your way. As the urge rises and becomes stronger and stronger, the wave gets higher and higher until it crests. Now imagine yourself riding that wave to shore. While watching and surfing the wave, notice what happens to it, if it gets higher and stronger, or if it's getting slower and weaker. When it gets weaker, imagine yourself sliding into shore on your surfboard and when it begins to build again, imagine yourself back out there riding the wave. Do this repeatedly for about ten minutes, or until you feel confident that you can handle the urge and will not act on it. At the end of the exercise, write down the strength of your urge on a scale from 0 to 10. Also on a scale of 0-10, write down how much you feel you can handle your urge. There are three important steps to keep in mind about this skill:

- Write down only the important consequences

- Memorize your list of consequences so that you can use it anytime you need it or just make a copy that you can carry with you;

- Pay rapt attention to the negative consequences of the behavior in question and use this strategy to motivate yourself to choose a different path when stressed out.

Stress affects everyone, we get irritated and a bit on edge many days. Adding anxiety problems to it can make it overwhelming. Taking care of yourself on a regular basis helps replenish your resources, which in turn helps to reduce stress. You can also reduce the impact of stress with the use of self-soothing and other calming techniques.

In conclusion, mindfulness, urge surfing, and concentrating on the consequences of your behaviors before taking action can help prevent you from worsening a situation by acting on your stress or aggravation. Some of the dialectical behavior therapy skills described in this chapter will hopefully help you to manage and reduce some of your stressors. In the following chapter, we will discuss strategies for managing worry and rumination.

Chapter 4 - DBT And Worry

All human beings worry. At some point in life, everyone reading this book has faced worry and are very familiar with it. Some worry more than others and sometimes you may worry more or less. However and whatever form your worry takes, it is a common experience for everyone. You really can't avoid it. People have been trained from an early age to focus all their attention on the future, what they want to achieve in future, where they need to be, and so on. Coupled with the unpredictability of life, how stressful and anxious life can be, this is the perfect recipe for worry.

Why Worry?

Just like all other behaviors that people have, worry serves a purpose. It is not random. Worry develops and stays for a reason. Worry is negative thoughts focused on the future of a number of different things like your job, family, health, or finances. Worry is also "what if" thinking. For instance, people worry about things like What if I can't pay my health insurance next month? or What if I lose my job? Worrying is essentially identifying a problem that could occur later in the future. This could be a useful process in some ways. Worry serves a useful function if it motivates some kind of preventive action, helps you come up with a solution to the problem, or just prepares you for an upcoming negative event. For these reasons, many people say that their worry is actually helpful. However, regardless of how helpful some people find their worry, more often than not, worry simply causes more anxiety. This is how it works. Future occurrences are unpredictable and largely out of our control and so this will normally generate some anxiety. Due to this, we may begin to worry by trying to make things seem more predictable and controllable, reducing our anxiety and all its symptoms including increased heart rate in the short term.

When we worry, we are actually identifying a future problem that may or may not happen, which means that a solution may not be possible. Additionally, we are not sure if the solution we came up with will actually work. Worry takes the form of problem-solving without actually solving, identifying a problem without really being able to arrive at a definite solution. As a result of this, our anxiety will return, often with increasing force, such that we will worry even more.

Several symptoms of anxiety are actually normal, everyday occurrences. As earlier mentioned, everybody worries to some extent, but worry can become so intense for some that it feels uncontrollable and is constantly occurring, interfering greatly with their ability to engage in positive and meaningful activities.

In this case, a person may develop GAD.

Worry in GAD and Other Anxiety Disorders

Generalized anxiety disorder is more common than people realize. A survey conducted on a large number of people across the United States showed that about 4 percent of people suffered from GAD at some point in their lifetimes. The primary feature of GAD is constant and uncontrollable worry about several events or activities. In GAD, a person also experiences at least three symptoms of chronic anxiety.

You must exhibit excessive and uncontrollable worry in addition to three of the symptoms previously listed, and these symptoms also need to interfere with some parts of your life for you to be diagnosed with GAD.

Note that just because you worry doesn't mean you have GAD. Worry doesn't have to be a result of GAD to cause problems in your life. Worry can stand on its own and is also seen in other anxiety symptoms, such as panic attacks. For example, people who have panic disorder may worry about the future panic attacks. Someone with social anxiety disorder may worry about future social situations and how they will handle those situations while people with PTSD may worry about how to stay safe. Regardless of what people worry about, the function and consequences of worry are the same. When we worry, we attempt to avoid anxiety or other unpleasant emotions, a strategy that backfires in the long term but is effective in the short term. Most people who worry discover that their anxiety actually increases over time and they miss out on the pleasant parts of their lives in the present moment when they worry excessively.

Features and Consequences of Worry

Worry can affect your life in major ways. We will discuss some common features of worry, alongside some of its negative consequences, while also taking you through some dialectical behavior therapy skills that may be effective in addressing certain features or consequences.

The Vicious Cycle of Worry: Getting Caught Up in Our Thoughts

Worry is quite difficult to let go as it has a tendency to grab our attention. Worry makes us aware of problems that may occur in the future and no matter how unlikely these occurrences may be, they are definitely things we don't want to happen. So it is only normal that we would want to dwell on these thoughts and try to think up a solution. However, the problem with worrying over a future occurrence is that most times, there is no solution and there also may not really be a problem. The anxiety we feel may be the cause of these worries about potential problems while trying to establish some form of predictability and control.

When worrying, people have a tendency to get caught up in their thoughts, and doing this, maintains the worry cycle. Some people try to manage this by attempting to suppress their worrisome thoughts. This suppression may be successful in the short run, but not in the long run, as those worrisome thoughts will return, possibly even stronger or more intense. When people tell themselves not to think about something, they increase the likelihood of thinking about it. Trying not to think about something, including worries, will naturally remind you of the very thoughts you don't want to have. This is due to the fact that you have to be on guard constantly to be sure that the thought isn't entering your mind, and by looking for it, your chances of finding it will increase.

Although it may seem as if trying not to worry is the simple solution to managing your worry and stopping the worry cycle, just know that it will not work. Attempting to eliminate worrisome thoughts will only make them stronger. Rather, dialectical behavior therapy mindfulness skills offer a better alternative to help manage your worry and respond to these thoughts.

Noticing Thoughts Without Attaching To Them

Worry thoughts get stuck in our minds, they don't pass through our minds and slip back out, they just stay. In fact, this is the reason we get attached to them. We pick them up as they enter our minds and then find it difficult to get rid of them. Therefore, the dialectical behavior therapy mindfulness skill of noticing thoughts without attaching to, acting or reacting to them is one of the most useful skills when dealing with worrisome thoughts. The basic idea is to allow thoughts slide out of your mind the same way the nonstick Teflon coating on pans lets food slide out of it after cooking. You know how the food tends to stick to the bottom of the pan and is difficult to remove from the pan in one piece when you're using a pan without a Teflon coating? If we don't practice having a "Teflon coated mind," worrisome thoughts stick to our minds instead of sliding out. Hence, the purpose of this mindfulness skill is to allow your worrisome thoughts slide in and out of your mind without actually getting stuck.

A way to do this is to imagine that you're placing each of the thoughts that passes through your mind onto a conveyor belt. Conveyor belts operate at a steady speed, transporting objects slowly across a room. In the same manner, imagine all of your thoughts moving slowly and steadily across your mind. Don't try to make the speed of the conveyor belt faster or try to take thoughts off the conveyor belt, simply notice every thought passing through your mind, one after the other. If at a point, you observe that the thoughts have begun piling up on one another on the belt, or that the conveyor belt stalls, or your thoughts start falling off the belt, just notice that experience and gently refocus your attention on the conveyor belt, replacing each thought on the belt and keeping your mind's eye on it as it moves through. Spend at least five minutes per a day practicing this exercise.

Labeling Thoughts As Thoughts

Another way you can deal with worrisome thoughts is through the DBT mindfulness skill of labeling your experience. A major reason why humans get immensely attached to and involved in worrisome thoughts is because we view these thoughts as literally true. We believe our thoughts and make them the truth rather than identifying these worries for why they simply are; thoughts generated by our minds, that may or may not be true. So when you label a thought as just a thought, it helps to keep you from buying into your thoughts or reacting as if they were true. This skill will help you understand that worries are just thoughts created by your mind, and not truths or a prediction of future occurrences. The next time you have a worrisome thought, make sure you label it as just a thought. For instance, instead of thinking to yourself I'm going to fail this class or I'll lose my job, describe these thoughts as merely thoughts by consciously thinking things like I feel like I'm going to lose my job or I'm having the thought that I will fail this class. This approach helps you to clearly label your thoughts as they are - just thoughts generated by your mind - and will enable you retreat from your worries and not immerse yourself in them as if they were the truth.

Not Being in the Present Moment

One other consequence of worry is how it removes us from the present moment. As earlier mentioned, worrying thoughts are focused on the future, which means getting caught up in these thoughts can cause you to miss out on present experience. Being constantly caught in these thoughts about the future means you may miss out on some very pleasant and rewarding experiences in the present moment. When you are not fully involved in the present moment, you often feel as if your life isn't meaningful and rewarding. And this is true in some ways. Not being fully present as you go about your day means you probably aren't living a rewarding enough life as you could be if you were fully involved in happenings around you. Being partially present in your life will prevent you from fully experiencing the meaningful aspects of your life and can begin to feel as if you are on autopilot.

Noticing And Labeling Your Experience In The Moment

You can combat this consequence of worry by using the dialectical behavior therapy skills of noticing and labeling your experience to enable you be in touch with your present experience. Focus your attention on noticing and describing what you are doing in the moment instead of getting caught up in your head and thoughts.

Throwing Yourself Into Your Experiences

Yet another skill to help you stay in touch with the present moment is the DBT mindfulness skill of throwing yourself fully into what you are doing presently. The purpose of this skill is to immerse yourself in your experiences and completely connect with them. This skill keeps you grounded in the present moment as well as helping you derive the utmost benefit from what you are doing.

So, when next you notice you are getting too involved in your worries, practice refocusing your full attention and awareness on whatever you are doing at the moment. Throw yourself into the experience. If you get distracted by your thoughts, just notice it, and then gently redirect your attention to the present moment and activity at hand.

Emotional Avoidance

Worry may be momentarily effective in helping you distract yourself from your anxiety. Reports made by people who struggle with worry states that their worry helps distract them from other more emotionally distressing areas of their lives. Allowing yourself to worry may feel like you are making efforts to manage your emotions, but is ultimately just a form of emotional avoidance. Worry really does nothing to address your emotions. Just like all other forms of emotional avoidance, it will fail in the long term, which will cause those emotions to come back even stronger. Then, worry is actually counterproductive and may cause your feelings to seem confusing, and unpredictable. Provided that people use worry as an attempt - however unsuccessful - to manage unpleasant emotions, a better alternative to using worry is to learn healthy and more effective emotion regulation skills, particularly ones that increase your acceptance of emotions. Following are some exercises that focus on ways of reducing emotional avoidance.

Mindfully Notice And Attend To Your Emotions

If you find that you often try to avoid or escape your emotions, then sometimes the best bet for you is to purposely notice your emotions, focus on them, weigh them, accept them for what they are, and allow them come and go. Using worry to deal with your emotions can be quite unproductive, so instead, mindfully notice them and you might just discover that your anxiety or fear or any other emotions you were running from m are not quite as bad as you thought they were. You might even come to understand that it's perfectly alright to experience these emotions and that you don't have to do always do something to get rid of them.

When next you catch yourself worrying, the following steps can be useful.

Pay close attention to what you feel in your body when you feel a particular emotion. This is to help you avoid becoming caught up in your thoughts and to try not to escape or avoid the emotions you feel. All you have to do is to bring your attention to the physical sensations of the emotions you are experiencing. You'll come across this type of exercise again in another chapter later on, where the book discusses how to deal with overwhelming emotions associated with post-traumatic stress.

However, this exercise is much more focused on worry, so it is helpful for whenever you start to worry.

- The first step is to recognize when you're worrying. After recognizing, tell yourself, Okay, I'm worrying again.

- For the second step, concentrate your attention on your body and observe any emotional sensations that you can identify. You might notice a tenseness in your muscles, hard and fast heartbeat, a feeling of nausea or butterflies in your stomach. Whatever you may be feeling, just concentrate on it and notice it. Train your attention on your body and if your mind is getting distracted by other things or you notice that worrisome thoughts are crawling into your mind, gently redirect your attention back to your body. Don't let yourself get entangled in your worrisome thoughts. Simply notice them and bring your mind back to your body repeatedly.

- Try labeling or naming your emotion, whatever it may be, whether anger, anxiety, fear, dread, annoyance, shame, irritation, or sadness. Understand that it's okay to feel what you feel, your emotion won't kill you, and simply leave the emotion there for as long as it stays there. Try to watch or notice it with curiosity. View your emotions as an ocean wave cresting and dissolving on the shore. Observe how fleeting emotions can be; one minute they're there and the next, they're gone. Emotions are normal, you don't need to avoid or escape them by all means.

Ensure that you practice all the skills that have been discussed in this book regularly. Take your time. Worry can be extremely difficult to manage usually because it feels as if it's effective momentarily. Worrisome thoughts are also quite good at stealing your attention. So, effective use of these skills will require some time and practice. Regardless of the difficulty it may pose, strengthening your connection with the present moment and turning off that autopilot can prove incredibly rewarding and meaningful for you.

In conclusion, keep in mind that the goal here is not to get rid of worry or never allow yourself to think about the future that would be impossible and pointless anyway. Rather, it's more effective to commit to knowing when you are getting entangled in your worry and then redirect your attention to the present moment, enabling you to use some healthier emotion regulation skills to deal with your anxiety or any other unpleasant emotion you may be feeling.

Chapter 5 - Flashbacks, Nightmares, and Other Traumatic Stress Symptoms

Research has discovered that many people (over half, in fact) will encounter a traumatic event at one point in their lives, and after this traumatic experience, people are at high risk of developing a range of anxiety-related symptoms. The particular sets of ensuing symptoms after a traumatic event are known as post-traumatic stress symptoms. Post-traumatic stress symptoms are usually extremely debilitating, they affect your relationships and ability to concentrate and stay focused negatively, disturb your sleep, and impact how much pleasure you derive from activities that you used to enjoy. Later on in the chapter, we will discuss some dialectical behavior therapy skills that are helpful for managing some post-traumatic stress symptoms. Before doing that, let's give you a quick overview of all the symptoms that can make up a post-traumatic stress response.

Post-Traumatic Stress Symptoms

Post-traumatic stress symptoms refers to a set of symptoms that ensues after a traumatic event. Several types of events could be considered as traumatic, events such as being a victim or witnessing physical or sexual assault, surviving or witnessing a motor vehicle accident, exposure to combat, being informed of a loved one's unexpected death, or experiencing a life-threatening illness. These symptoms can be classified into three different groups:

- Re-experiencing symptoms

- Avoidance and emotional numbing symptoms,

- Hyperarousal symptoms.

Let's review some of the specific symptoms that are in each group:

Re-experiencing Symptoms

Re-experiencing symptoms are ones that make people relive or be constantly reminded of the traumatic event that happened to them. There are five re-experiencing symptoms that people can experience after a traumatic experience:

- Frequent and intrusive thoughts or memories about the

traumatic experience.

- Recurring nightmares about the traumatic experience.

- Acting or feeling as though they were going through the traumatic event again. This is usually called a flashback - will be discussed in more detail.

- Experiencing distress after coming into contact with any reminder of the traumatic event. Such reminders may include thoughts about the event, a person, exposure to an object, a place, or any situation that triggers memories of the traumatic event.

- Experiencing bodily arousal such as an increased heart rate after coming into contact with a reminder of the traumatic event.

Avoidance and Emotional Numbing Symptoms

As expected, the re-experiencing symptoms after a traumatic event can be quite upsetting, therefore, it's not uncommon for people to do all sorts to try to prevent such symptoms from being triggered. These attempts are the avoidance symptoms that people experience after a traumatic event. Additionally, the fear, anxiety, and arousal that accompanies a traumatic event can also reduce a person's ability to derive pleasure from once enjoyable activities or even experience a connection with others. It is almost as if a person's ability to experience positive emotions is blocked, unlike how more unpleasant emotions are easily experienced. These are known as symptoms of emotional numbing. People experience seven avoidance and emotional numbing symptoms after a traumatic event.

- Attempts to avoid or suppress thoughts or feelings connected with the traumatic event.

- Endeavors to avoid all people, activities, places that may serve as a reminder of a traumatic event.

- Have difficultly recollecting vital parts of the traumatic event.

- Loss of interest in activities or things that they once found enjoyable.

- A feeling of disconnection or detachment from loved ones.

- Finding it difficult to experience the full range of emotions.

- Feeling as if life will be cut short in some way.

Hyperarousal Symptoms

People often experience constant bodily arousal after a

traumatic event and this can have a number of negative effects like concentration problems, difficulty sleeping, or constantly feeling on guard and on edge. These consequences are all under the larger category of hyperarousal symptoms that people can experience after a traumatic event. There are five symptoms of hyperarousal:

- Difficulty falling asleep or staying asleep.

- Overly irritable feelings or having angry outbursts.

- Difficulty concentrating or staying focused.

- Constantly feeling on guard or alert, as though there were some kind of threat present (referred to as hypervigilance).

- Constant feeling jumpy or being easily startled.

Is It Post-Traumatic Stress Disorder?

After experiencing a traumatic event, only some of the people actually develop enough of the previously listed symptoms to meet the criteria for post-traumatic stress disorder (PTSD). A person is diagnosed with PTSD when they meet a particular number of symptoms from each of the previous categories of symptoms at least thirty days after the traumatic event. In addition, the symptoms also have to negatively impact a person's life. Regardless, even if a person is not experiencing enough of the symptoms to qualify for a PTSD diagnosis, they may still encounter some negative consequences as a result of their symptoms. Therefore, even if you think you won't meet the criteria for a PTSD diagnosis, as long as you are experiencing any of the symptoms previously listed due to a traumatic event, you must take steps to manage them in healthy manner. Doing this might help avoid the development of PTSD and lessen the negative effects of the post-traumatic stress symptoms on you.

DBT Skills to Deal with Post-Traumatic Stress Symptoms

Here we discuss some of the characteristics, the consequences of post-traumatic stress symptoms, and ways that certain dialectical behavior therapy skills may be effective in managing those symptoms and their consequences. Keep in mind as you read through the different symptoms discussed, that not all may be represented. A person can develop a number of anxiety-related symptoms after a traumatic event that aren't specific to a post-traumatic stress response. For instance, some people develop panic attacks or worry after experiencing a traumatic event. If the anxiety-related symptoms you're experiencing aren't listed here, panic attacks or worry, look through the rest of the book. You will probably find them represented in other chapters, with dialectical behavior therapy skills for dealing with them.

Using Mindfulness and Distress Tolerance to Manage Intrusive Experiences such as Thoughts, Nightmare and Flashbacks

Here will discuss intrusive experiences, which are quite common among persons who have encountered trauma. They're called intrusive experiences because in a manner of speaking, the experiences intrude into your brain without an invitation from you. Such experiences are flashbacks, intrusive thoughts or memories and nightmares.

It is very common for intrusive thoughts or memories about a traumatic event to pop up, and the accompanying anxiety and fear can greatly interfere with your everyday life. There are many things that you might encounter throughout your day that can be quick triggers of thoughts and memories of a traumatic event. Things like sounds, specific places, newspaper articles, smells, television shows, conversations, and people who are connected in some form to the event, or remind you of it can cause an onslaught of memories about that traumatic event. Due to this, these thoughts and memories can be quite unpredictable and can catch you off guard. Intrusive thoughts and memories can also distract your attention from your normal daily activities, thereby making it difficult for you to focus. Even more, the intense pain and distress they bring can be distracting and overwhelming.

Another very common symptom that develops after a traumatic event are nightmares. Nightmares can negatively influence your sleep and anxiety levels. No one knows for certain the exact cause of nightmares; however, some people believe that problems with regulating emotions during the day may be a contributor to nightmares. It could be the case that your brain is trying to process or deal with emotions that you were unable to work through in the day. So, by learning to regulate your emotions and lessen vulnerability to distress more effectively, you may just be able to reduce the number of times you get nightmares.

Unlike nightmares, flashbacks happen when you're awake and you feel as though a traumatic event were reoccurring. At times, someone might act out a traumatic event as though it were happening presently. As if experiencing the trauma in the first place wasn't bad enough, your brain sometimes forces you to relive it all over again. The severity of a flashback ranges from being caught up in thoughts or memories - similar to daydreaming - to being entirely unaware of one's surroundings and losing all sense of time and place, which is sometimes referred to as dissociation. Also, people may hallucinate during a flashback. Flashbacks can be a truly horrific experience regardless of its severity. A person who is caught up in a flashback may feel disconnected from the present moment and may find it difficult to extract themselves from it, thereby increasing their anxiety and fear.

All of these experiences (intrusive thoughts, flashbacks, and nightmares) are similar in one area - they're all intrusive - and so the types of skills used to manage them are extremely similar too. Almost the same. Mindfulness skills may be the first line of defense when handling intrusive experiences. All the experiences require that your brain brings back these upsetting past experiences in forms of intrusive thoughts and memories, flashbacks, or nightmares. Therefore, a remedy for these symptoms is to concentrate your mind in the real, present moment. If you can achieve this, it will be more difficult for the intrusive thoughts or memories to creep in and overwhelm you. As real as a flashback may seem, remember the events are actually not happening right now. If you can focus your mind on present happenings, you might be more equipped to ride out the flashback until it ends. Nightmares may have you waking up in cold or hot sweat or find yourself doing things that you'd never do normally. In these instances, focusing your attention on present happenings can effectively calm your mind, lessen the storm of ensuing upsetting emotions after the nightmare, and secure you in the present moment. When dealing with intrusive thoughts, you might also be able to take some of the power out of the thoughts if you can take the spotlight of your attention out of your head and into your immediate experience.

When you practice mindfulness, you can choose to focus on either your internal experiences like bodily sensations, thoughts, and emotions or on external experiences, like tactile sensations, sights and sounds. But when dealing with upsetting, intrusive experiences, focusing on external experiences is the most effective way to start with mindfulness. Sometimes, when experiencing a nightmare or flashback, the onslaught of internal bodily arousal, images, thoughts and sensations is too much to manage. And so paying attention to your external environment and external physical sensations is the best way to anchor yourself in the present.

Notice and Describe Your Experiences, and Immerse Yourself in Your Activities

<u>Conduct a reality check</u> when you are in the middle of a flashback or dealing with a bunch of intrusive thoughts or memories, or you've just woken up from a nightmare. Take a step back and observe, then state the problem clearly.

For example:

I have been having nightmares about ...

I have just had a flashback or intrusive thoughts about ...

If you are having a flashback, keep in mind that whatever seems to be happening is not the reality. If it's a nightmare, remind yourself that it was just a nightmare and is not actually happening. For intrusive thoughts, tell yourself that they are mere thoughts, nothing more.

You can try writing or describing what exactly is happening to yourself as a reality check.

<u>Notice your experiences and describe what you feel</u>. Switch on the lights in the room if they're not on. Sit up in an alert position, with your feet placed on the ground. If your mind wanders during this exercise, it's perfectly okay; minds wander. Keep returning your attention to whatever you're observing as many times as you need to. That's the point of mindfulness. Practice it for about five to twenty minutes, or as long you need to feel more anchored in the present moment.

a. Take a step back and focus your attention, then describe how you feel. Now bring your attention to the sensations of your feet on the ground or floor. Just notice what the bottoms of your feet feel like. Notice any sensations of pressure, pain, temperature, tension, or relaxation. Notice how the surface of the insides of your shoes feel like if you're wearing one. If not, notice what the surface of the floor or ground feels like. Bring your focus to how your bottom feels like on whatever you're sitting on. Just notice any sensations of sitting. Keep reminding yourself that you are here in the present, and that the flashback is just a flashback, not reality or that the nightmare is over. Next, place your hands on your knees and notice the feelings in the palms of your hands. Pay attention to see if you can also notice any other tactile sensations.

b. Notice and describe your environment. If you are going through a flashback, try your best to look through it at what you can really see in your immediate surroundings. Try to ignore any visions of events, people, or places related to the flashback. Bring your gaze to the floor and notice what you see there. Scan the floor for a minute or two and notice what you see there. Now, raise your eyes up to the walls and pay attention to what you see there. Notice the wall colors, any artwork on the walls, door frames, door knobs, lighting fixtures, and so on. Simply take a mental step back and notice these things. You should also look at the ceiling, and pay attention to the textures, objects, colors, you see there. Now, bring your gaze to the chair, bed, or floor you are sitting on.

c. Step back, observe, and describe what you can hear. Listen with rapt attention to anything you hear where you are sitting, or outside. Gently ignore any sounds from the flashback. Just focus on exactly what you hear. For example, you might notice the sounds of your own breathing, people talking, the birds, the rain, or the wind. Just notice what you hear.

Throw yourself into an activity. Immerse your mind into an activity in the present moment. Remember distress tolerance skills in chapter 3? Here is where you will combine distraction or self-soothing skills and throwing yourself into what you are doing right now. You first need to decide if you need soothing or distraction. To help you choose, determine if your nervous system is all wired up and you feel tense or feel bodily arousal, if this is the case, self-soothing might be your best option. Contrarily, if you feel your mind going back to the nightmare, flashback or intrusive thoughts, you might want to choose distraction. You can never go wrong with either, so you can decide to try both.

Here are some tips on throwing yourself into your activities:

- Immerse yourself into the activity so that you're completely involved in it.

- Engage in the activity with your entire body, mind, and soul.

- Do whatever it is with energy and vigor, and whenever your mind wanders, continue throwing yourself back in, as though you were jumping back into a swimming pool every time you crawled out.

If distraction is your choice, pick an activity that will direct your attention away from your worries. So, choose something you find interesting or stimulating like the following:

- Physical exercise such as running, an energetic walk,

doing push-ups, sit-ups, yoga or aerobics.

- Do crosswords, solve puzzles or sudokus.

- See and interact with other people

- Shopping

- Read a very engaging book or article

- Get out of your home and hop on the bus to go somewhere

- Do arts, crafts, or other hobbies

- Get some work or studying done

- Eating - not too much.

- Try doing something that generates strong, distracting sensations, like showering with alternating cold and hot water or eating spicy food.

If you choose to use self-soothing, engage in calming activity. When dealing with stressful events like nightmares or flashbacks, it's best to seek a little comfort or soothing after or during. Therefore, choose something comforting or soothing to you, something calming to your mind and body. Below are some examples of activities that can soothe your various senses:

- Sound: Listen to calming, soothing music like classical music. A great hack to find such music is to get the types of music recommended for women in labor.

- <u>Sight</u>: Look at art, watch a nature show that's calming. Don't watch anything with lions or other predators attacking unsuspecting animals. Try someplace where you can see nature or beauty, if you can't, look at photographs of such places or find soothing photos or scenes of nature on the Internet.

- <u>Smell</u>: Light aromatherapy candles or incense. Smell flowers, sit in a bath with scented oils, make a cup of coffee or tea and just smell it or smell fresh coffee beans.

- <u>Touch</u>: Wear soft, soothing materials; wrap yourself in your favorite blanket; have a calming, warm shower; run your fingers all over something with a nice, calming texture; have a massage done or get your hair done.

- <u>Taste</u>: Eat comfort food; eat food with a calming, comforting taste or texture; or just eat some candy or chocolate slowly and mindfully.

Using Opposite Action to Reduce Avoidance

Post-traumatic stress symptoms can be extremely distressing, leading to elevated levels of anxiety and fear, sometimes even shame, guilt, and anger. Hence, it is unsurprising that people suffering from these symptoms or emotions try to avoid them and situations that might awaken those symptoms. Some people may avoid large crowds, enclosed places, new people (such as going on dates), or high places. This system of avoidance is usually effective in the short term, as it helps people to avoid anything that may trigger unpleasant memories, thoughts, and emotions linked with a particular traumatic event. But in the long term, avoidance leads to greater distress or increased detachment from loved ones or situations they care about. Which means, a person might begin to feel trapped or caged in by the symptoms and the resultant avoidance behaviors.

The dialectical behavior therapy emotion regulation skill of the opposite action is a great way to prevent avoidance. As seen in chapter 3, opposite action involves doing the exact opposite of what you feel like doing at the moment when you're feeling a particular emotion. In post-traumatic stress, the emotion is often fear. We will go on to discuss how opposite action can help you gain freedom from fear and avoidance.

This is how opposite action works. If for instance, you were assaulted by a male acquaintance whom you met in a park during the day a few years ago, and because of this, you have grown scared of parks and places with trees and bushes, so you avoid walking in such places. Also, you might have begun avoiding walking or traveling any distance outside on your own, even during the day, and you may generally avoid men. Following all these, you find that your life has grown secluded and your world narrower, since you avoid so many people and places. Opposite action functions by helping your brain determine which of these places or people are not dangerous and don't require you to avoid them. Once your brain successfully makes that connection, your fear begins to lessen and you are more open to things or people you previously avoided. Your life opens up so that you gain more freedom to go anywhere you want to and do what you want without fear.

In this case, opposite action would involve intentionally doing the opposite of what your fear prompts you to do. If your fear prompts you to avoid riding the bus in the middle of the day because you might get assaulted on the bus, opposite action would involve intentionally getting on the bus during the day as many times as you can, so that your brain understands that it's safe to ride on the bus. If for example you're afraid of walking in a public park at noon, opposite action would involve walking in a public park at noon on purpose, multiple times until your fear lessens.

Now, you might be worried that you might actually get harmed or assaulted. Remember this important point about opposite action: only take opposite action for fear in instances where your fear will most likely not come true. Which means, you wouldn't choose to walk through a dangerous neighborhood at night. If walking through that neighborhood scares you, you probably have good reason to be afraid, and so avoiding that neighborhood is a good idea. Alternatively, you cannot be 100 percent certain that a situation will be safe. So, when you begin riding the bus or walking through a park, you should make sure that you'll probably be much more safe than unsafe.

For example, a woman who had been assaulted in the park exact situation, but she loved running and the outdoors, and she didn't want to have to avoid parks for the rest of her life. So she took opposite action by visiting the park multiple times, but ensuring that she did so as safely as possible, e.g sticking to well-used trails and not listening to music while running.

Using Mindfulness to Manage Overwhelming Emotions and Problems Managing Emotions

Experiencing a traumatic event can have a huge impact on how you manage your emotions. Following a traumatic event, you may feel your emotions much more intensely, they may change suddenly and as previously discussed, sometimes after a traumatic event, people find it difficult to connect with positive emotional experiences. This is referred to as "emotional numbing." However, negative emotions such as anger, sadness, and fear may be experienced quite strongly and a person may feel consumed by these emotions, which may make emotions more difficult to manage.

When the intensity of an emotion is heightened, it can be much more difficult to cope with, tolerate, and manage that emotion. You may also find it harder to control your behavior when emotions are heightened. Their intensity makes it more likely that you will want to avoid those emotions as quickly as you can, which can make you more prone to engaging in impulsive behaviors. Impulsive behaviors are actions that you engage in quickly and rashly, sparing little thought for the potential consequences of that behavior. These behaviors include alcoholism, deliberate self-harm such as cutting or burning yourself and binge eating. Regardless of the fact that these behaviors are effective in the short term by rapidly lowering the intensity of an unpleasant emotion, they have been linked with several long-term negative consequences. Also, since they just suppress emotions rather than actually managing them, the emotion that you were trying to avoid will return even stronger.

Luckily, several dialectical behavior therapy skills have been designed to tolerate and manage intense emotional experiences. These skills may be especially useful for people who have experienced a traumatic event and are finding it difficult to manage or cope with intense, unpleasant emotions.

An effective way to cope with difficulty sitting with intense, negative emotions is mindfulness. In particular, a mindfulness skill can be especially helpful in this case. As explained by Dr. Marsha Linehan, who calls it the skill of mindfulness of current emotion, it involves simply taking a step back, noticing, and paying attention to the physical sensations you feel in your current emotional state. It may sound like a lot of pain and hard work but allowing yourself to enter into, watch, and experience your emotions, might make you more likely to achieve freedom from them.

At times, the only way to escape misery is to not try to escape misery. Rather, enter into and pay attention. Paying attention and mindfully noticing your emotions can better equip you to tolerate its unpleasant aspects, so that when next they arise, they are easier to manage and tolerate. As you do this repeatedly, you will find that emotions don't last forever; they just wax and wane without any influence from you to change or get rid of them. In addition, if you get to practice a lot simply by sitting with and taking care of your emotions and urges to avoid them, you just might be able to improve your ability to prevent yourself from using impulsive behaviors such as outbursts, drinking, doing drugs, self-harming, behaving recklessly to escape or avoid emotions.

Pay Attention to and Notice Your Emotional State

When next you have time and you experience a moderately strong emotion, look for a quiet place to sit in an alert, upright position, with feet placed flat on the ground.

Bring your attention to your body, and observe where exactly in you feel that emotion. Scan your body from head to toe, and pay attention to the sensations in every part of your body as you proceed. Spend around ten seconds on each part of your body, just step back in your mind, pay attention, and notice your sensations. This routine is quite similar to the body scan technique developed by Dr. Jon Kabat-Zinn, who is an expert on mindfulness-based treatment.

After scanning your body, focus on those parts of your body where you feel the emotion. For example, you might feel an adrenaline rush in your chest, tension in your shoulders and neck, or a racing sensation in your heart. Locate and focus on those areas where you feel the sensations of your emotion. Watch how the sensations rise and fall like you would watch a wave rise and fall on the ocean.

Continue to focus on the physical sensations of your emotion without trying to escape or avoid them. Don't try to avoid, escape or push the emotion away, and don't try to distract your mind with other activities or thoughts. You don't need to avoid. Just watch the physical sensations as though they were waves on the ocean, notice how they change, how they increase or decrease. Keep this up for about five to ten minutes, or until the emotion subsides.

Dealing with Relationship Problems

Many people develop problems with interpersonal relationships after they experience a traumatic event. They often feel detached from people. Shame and guilt are common emotions that follow a traumatic event, which can actively interfere with interpersonal relationships, making it difficult for them to achieve intimacy with loved ones.

Anger and irritability are also common post-traumatic stress symptoms, which can also interfere with relationships. After a traumatic event has happened, a person may find it harder to control their anger or aggressive behavior, which may cause friends and loved ones to maintain distance or feel as if they had to be extra careful around you. While some people try to avoid all forms of conflict after a traumatic event. They may be unwilling to express their needs or desires in a relationship out of fear of not wanting to upset the person or bringing up an argument or they may be scared that loved ones will leave due to their post-traumatic stress symptoms. However, if you are unable to express your needs, you may begin to feel resentment, or miss out on opportunities to get the social support you need, which is a crucial factor in helping you recover from a traumatic event.

Post-traumatic stress symptoms can be extremely challenging to manage on a daily basis, hence it is important that you possess some tools for dealing with these experiences and lessening their negative influence on your life. Several DBT skills like mindfulness and distress tolerance skills for grounding yourself in the moment and handling flashbacks and nightmares, mindfulness of your emotions to help you regulate and tolerate emotions, opposite action for combating avoidance, and interpersonal effectiveness skills to help you identify and communicate your needs can be helpful. All of these recommendations and exercises should be of great help to you. You might also consider trying some other skills discussed in chapters 2, 4, and throughout the rest of the book, to help you manage problems related to post-traumatic stress. The next chapter will discuss the symptoms of panic attacks and panic disorder, and how to use dialectical behavior therapy to effectively manage them.

Chapter 6 - DBT And Panic Attacks

Panic attacks are the sudden experience of intense fear or absolute terror that are the major symptom of panic disorder and occurs in majority of anxiety disorders. However, if you recollect from the first chapter, panic attacks are actually quite common, even in people who don't have a diagnosis of anxiety disorder. They can be quite frightening and may hugely affect a person's life. But luckily, dialectical behavior therapy skills can be incredibly useful in serving as a cushion to the impact of a panic attack and may be able to eliminate panic attacks entirely. Before we delve into the specific dialectical behavior therapy skills that are great for panic attacks, it is important that we fully understand what panic attacks are, their causes, and how they can impact a person's life.

What Are Panic Attacks?

If you've ever had a panic attack, you probably know what a panic attack is and what it feels like. A panic attack is incredibly stronger than anxiety or fear, it is basically your body's fight-or-flight alarm going off suddenly. It is a "false alarm" because your body is essentially informing you that you are faced by some kind of immediate danger, even if there's no imminent threat. Later on, we'll discuss why this may happen. A person who experiences a panic attack is bombarded with immensely strong feelings of fear, terror, or discomfort that rise and peak quickly and excruciatingly. A panic attack can be expected or unexpected. Unexpected panic attacks are also sometimes referred to as "out of the blue," spontaneous, or knee jerk. A large number of the first panic attacks that people experience happen without prior warning.

With no undue influence, a panic attack lasts just a few minutes, even though it may feel as if it would go on forever. However, your response to the panic attack can influence and determine how long the panic attack lasts. There's next to nothing you can do to help or stop a panic attack except to let it run its course. Basically, you have to wait for that false alarm to turn off. If you attempt to avoid the symptoms of a panic attack or suppress them, that alarm can endure for longer or even get stronger sometimes.

Of course, it's a normal reaction that a person would want to avoid a panic attack whenever possible, as it is an unpleasant experience. But ultimately, trying to escape or avoid a panic attack just makes it stronger and longer. So, as scary as a panic attack can be, the sensible things is to simply ride it out until it's over. Later on, we will discuss some DBT skills that may ease the discomfort of a panic attack.

While having a panic attack, people may feel a variety of bodily sensations, including shortness of breath, increased heart rate, sweating, and dizziness. They also usually have some fearful thoughts like I'm going crazy or I'm going to die during the attack. As a matter of fact, many people on their first experience of panic attacks think that they are having a heart attack, and they visit the emergency room, because the physical sensations and fear that come with a panic attack are achingly intense.

Below are some common sensations that people experience during a panic attack, with the most common ones being increased heart rate, trembling, dizziness, and fear of losing control. To be diagnosed as a panic attack, a person must experience at least four of the symptoms described next. A person with fewer than four of these symptoms, may only be experiencing what is known as limited-symptom panic attack. Limited-symptom panic attacks are not as common as standard panic attacks and are generally less intense, but they may still have some of the same negative consequences of a standard panic attack. Regardless of whether a person experiences full-symptom or limited-symptom panic attacks, it is vital that you be aware of the symptoms you usually experience during a panic attack. Having this information will allow you to tailor the described DBT skills to these particular symptoms.

Panic Attacks in Anxiety Disorders

Now, experiencing panic attacks does not automatically mean you have an anxiety disorder. However, people who have anxiety disorders commonly have panic attacks, and of course, sudden panic attacks are the central defining feature of panic disorder. Outside of panic disorder, panic attacks are usually expected or triggered by something in the immediate environment. If for example, a person with a specific phobia may have a panic attack when confronted with the source of their phobia, such as an enclosed space, a snake, or high grounds. A person with social anxiety disorder may have a panic attack when they're in a social situation where they may face criticism or negative reviews. A panic attack may occur in PTSD if a person comes in contact with a reminder of the traumatic event. So, as seen, the actual difference in panic attacks across the anxiety disorders is what triggers them. Otherwise, there aren't much differences in what having a panic attack feels like or its consequences. Alongside talking about dialectical behavior therapy skills for panic attacks, we will also discuss panic attacks in more general terms, instead of discussing it within any particular anxiety disorder.

Where Do Panic Attacks Come From?

Before going into dialectical behavior therapy skills, let's have some information on where panic attacks originate from and how they develop. There are many schools of thought on this topic, but here, we will review just a couple of the more well-supported ones.

A Biological Theory of Panic Attacks

Some believe that people who are predisposed to be hypersensitive to carbon dioxide levels in their bodies are more likely to develop panic attacks. Based on this theory, panic attacks are caused by a part of the brain that has undergone evolution to be on the look out for situations where a person may be in a situation where they can suffocate. This "look out or monitor" in the brain activates the alarm - a panic attack - when it detects an increase in the levels of carbon dioxide in the bloodstream. The monitor may also sound the alarm when a person is at risk of loss of oxygen, which would include any situation where someone feels trapped, as though they couldn't escape. There is some evidence for and against this theory, which likely means that a hypersensitivity to carbon dioxide explains why some people have panic attacks, but not others.

Psychological Theories of Panic Attacks

There are several psychological explanations for why panic attacks arise, but the basic theme of these theories is that panic attacks happen when people negatively assess, or judge, the bodily sensations that usually come with anxiety or panic attacks. The primary idea is that some people hold beliefs that symptoms related to anxiety, like certain thoughts or bodily sensations, will yield negative or even terrible consequences, and these beliefs then increase their chances of experiencing a panic attack. For instance, someone may believe that an increase in their heart rate is a sign that they will have a heart attack. This negative evaluation of such a normal bodily sensation can then make them fear that sensation, further intensifying the sensation and ultimately their anxiety. This cycle continues until their anxiety becomes so intense that they have a panic attack.

Also, people may try to avoid that feared sensation, which is quite an understandable reaction, but it usually only intensifies that sensation, and the vicious cycle continues. A person may develop the belief that the normal bodily sensations that accompany anxiety are harmful because of their upbringing or history with anxiety or it may be passed down through a person's genes and are therefore hardwired.

What Panic Attacks Look Like And Their Consequences

We'll review some common features of panic attacks and some of its negative consequences. We'll also walk you through some dialectical behavior therapy skills that may help address that particular feature or consequence.

Avoidance

Panic attacks and avoidance go well together such that when people experience a panic attack - whether it's expected or not - they often try their best to avoid the experience again. People who have expected or cued panic attacks may try to stay away from cues such as a feared object or situation that could trigger a panic attack. In unexpected panic attacks, people may try to prevent themselves from feeling the bodily sensations that come with a panic attack, like an increased heart rate, shortness of breath. For instance, some people may avoid exercising, drinking caffeine, sexual activity, eating heavy meals, just to make sure they don't do anything that could increase their heart rate. Some people may also use substances like alcohol to try to calm themselves and lower their chances of experience certain bodily sensations, like increased heart rate and muscle tension.

These strategies may be effective in the short term or work some of the time, but it's not possible to completely avoid bodily sensations, particularly those linked to anxiety. Therefore, such strategies as described above won't work, instead this type of avoidance usually contribute to the vicious cycle, which could eventually lead to the development of substance use or agoraphobia. People with agoraphobia have intense anxiety about situations where they find escape or help difficult such as, large crowds. Someone with agoraphobia will go to great lengths to avoid such situations and it may sometimes worsen to the extent that people don't feel safe outside of their homes. There are some skills that can help you with the avoidance that accompanies panic attacks.

Approaching Environmental Cues Of Panic Attacks

One of the most effective skills for dealing with avoidance among people with panic attacks is opposite action. As discussed in chapter 4, this skill helps you change emotions that may be hindering your way of your life by helping you respond to them differently. Although fear can be very useful, as it informs you of any threats around you, it can go a bit off-track and start to malfunction.

As mentioned, panic attacks are considered a false alarm given off by your body's alarm system, so one of the most helpful ways to handle the fear associated with panic attacks is to face your fear head-on. If the situations or objects that trigger panic attacks were truly dangerous, then it would be helpful to avoid them. But the problem is that these situations and objects are not inherently dangerous, and avoiding them will only worsen the panic. So approaching them head-on is the best way to deal with the fear and avoidance of these cues.

Now, this may sound counterintuitive, but approaching these cues and situations gives you the chance to realize that they are not inherently dangerous and may not always lead to a panic attack. If they do lead to a panic attack, it helps you learn that panic attacks themselves, as distressing and uncomfortable as they are will not lead to some catastrophic outcome. You realize that you can experience a panic attack and be okay, while you can also have the chance to practice other skills to ease you through the panic attack more quickly.

How does acting opposite to fear work? As earlier mentioned, the basic idea is to approach your fear over and over again. Approach any of the people, places, activities, experiences, or sensations that you are afraid of, and keep doing it until you are no longer afraid of facing those things.

- So as the first step, identify your panic attacks cue that you try to avoid. Start with expected or cued panic attacks. If you experience panic attacks as a result of specific cues around you, like certain objects or situations, the following exercise will help you learn how to apply the opposite acting to fear skill to these cues.

- Try to figure out what objects, situations, events, or things tend to trigger your expected panic attacks.

- Cues for someone with social phobia or an intense fear of facing negative evaluation by others may be social in nature and may include situations or events where you think you could be judged or evaluated, for example speaking in public, being around large groups of people, eating in front of others.

- If your phobia is specific, then the cues for your panic attacks may be specific to the things you are afraid of, e.g airplanes, elevators, enclosed spaces, spiders or snakes.

If you have PTSD, then your expected panic attacks cues may be ones that make you relive or remember your traumatic event, like sights or smells connected to your trauma.

Approaching Avoided Activities

When people experience unexpected panic attacks, it means that there is nothing particularly threatening around them that led to a panic attack, there's no specific object or situation that they can avoid in order to prevent a panic attack. Which means that people who experience unexpected panic attacks usually try to avoid feeling any of the bodily sensations that they've associated with panic attacks, like increased heart rate or shortness of breath.

Where is the problem with this? In addition to the fact that avoidance doesn't work in the long term, the major issue with attempting to avoid these common bodily sensations is that there are several activities that can cause your heart rate to increase or make you short of breath. And so to effectively avoid these sensations, you would need to severely limit your life.

Think about the kinds of things that increase your heart rate or cause you to be out of breath. Is it exercise, walking upstairs, having sex, watching an exciting or scary movie, consuming caffeine? This tells you that you would need to avoid all of these activities and many others to avoid these physical sensations. You would need to dramatically limit your life and avoid engaging in a ton of activities - some of which are actually enjoyable and healthy. And that can greatly reduce your quality of life.

Approaching The Bodily Sensations Associated With Panic Attacks

To address the avoidance tendency that comes with panic attacks, you can also approach the actual sensations associated with panic attacks. Up to this point, the exercises have focused on helping you deal with avoidance of situations, activities and objects, mainly because the avoidance of these activities and situations can be problematic. However, most of these forms of avoidance are actually all about preventing the bodily sensations that go with panic attacks. That's why you avoid doing so many of the activities and situations that you identified earlier. For many people, avoiding these bodily sensations fuels the rest of their avoidance behaviors, so, the best way to handle this type of avoidance is to approach these sensations. This may seem scary but rest assured that there are dialectical behavior therapy skills to guide you through it.

There are two skills that are particularly helpful. The first is using the skill of acting opposite to emotion previously described to approach each of the bodily sensations that you fear. The second set of skills that can guide your approach is the DBT mindfulness skills. As mentioned in the second chapter, DBT mindfulness skills can help you connect with internal experiences like your thoughts, feelings, and physical sensations that you often try to avoid. Also, since mindfulness skills are not only about what to do but how to, they can help you connect with these sensations such that you benefit from them. You can use the dialectical behavior therapy skill of noticing your experience without condemning it to help you approach the sensations associated with panic attacks. The first part of this skill simply involves noticing your internal experience without getting caught up in or reacting to it. So, rather than reacting to your bodily sensations or getting caught up in them, you would make it your goal in using this skill to just notice each sensation as it arises, without trying to push it away or cling to it. Simply focus all of your attention on observing any bodily sensations you experience, watching them arise and pass from one moment to the next.

The second part of this skill involves how exactly you should practice observing these sensations. As you notice your bodily sensations and observe them as they come and pass, ensure that you don't evaluate them. Notice them without judging or evaluating them and focus on simply noticing each sensation as it is, instead of judging it as bad or wrong. Remember that these sensations are simply a normal part of life; they're something that every human being experiences. Having this stance towards your experiences will help you realize that danger is not inherent in these sensations and will ultimately help you stop avoiding them.

Following is an exercise with some simple step-by-step instructions to help you notice your bodily sensations without judgment or evaluation.

1. First, look for a comfortable and quiet place to sit or lie down.

2. Close your eyes.

3. Concentrate on your breathing. Notice how you feel when breathing in and out. Breathe in and out and notice the

parts of your body that move.

4. Stretch your awareness outward to different areas of your body e.g your legs, arms, back, or neck. Just bring your attention to those parts of your body where you usually feel tension or experience the bodily sensations you're scared of.

5. Remember not to judge or evaluate those sensations. Instead try to notice them as mere sensations, nothing more.

6. If you notice yourself labeling or judging your sensations, note that evaluation or label, then continue noticing the sensations as simply sensations.

7. If judgments or thoughts distract you, make sure you notice it and then return your attention to noticing your sensations without judgement.

8. Practice concentrating your awareness on different areas of your body. Move your attention all over your entire body, and focus on observing the different bodily sensations without judging or labeling them.

9. Do this exercise for at least fifteen minutes at least a couple of times daily. When you start out, make sure you practice this exercise even when you don't feel especially anxious, in order to easily establish a new habit of

noticing your experience without passing judgment.

Catastrophic Beliefs on Bodily Sensations and Misinterpretations about it.

Panic attacks are sometimes triggered when people negatively label certain bodily sensations. For instance, people who feel certain anxiety-related bodily sensations may think that they are losing their mind or are dying. They may then misinterpret these normal bodily sensations as a sign that something is terribly wrong. Subsequently, these interpretations actually increase their chances of experiencing a panic attack. In simpler terms, if you believe that your racing heart or shortness of breath is a sign that you are going to have a heart attack, so you think you will feel better, or become even more anxious and afraid? Yea, your guess is as good as mine. Although these beliefs may be understandable, they are not necessarily true or accurate. So, believing that they are 100 percent accurate isn't incredibly helpful. However some good news is that you don't have to change these beliefs or avoid thinking about it before you can make progress in your recovery. There is a useful dialectical behavior therapy skill that can help deal with thought if this nature.

Labeling Your Experience Objectively As What It Is

The dialectical behavior therapy skill of objectively labeling your experience is one of the best skills for dealing with these types of thoughts. This skill helps you acknowledge and describe your experience only as what it is, a sensation as nothing more than a sensation, labeling a feeling as just a feeling, and a thought as only a thought. So, when next you find yourself having some of the bodily sensations that go with panic attacks, start labeling that experience objectively and put it into words. For instance, you can say to yourself, "my heart is starting to beat faster." My breathing is growing more shallow. I'm feeling short of breath. Then most importantly, if you notice any thoughts that go with that experience, ensure you label them as just thoughts. Rather than believing I'm having a heart attack or I'm about to die, describe them as mere thoughts by telling yourself that the thought "I'm having a heart attack" has crept into my mind or the thought "I'm about to die" has just entered my mind. This kind of approach to your thoughts and clearly labeling them as just thoughts that come into your mind will help you detach yourself from them and not believe them as though they were absolutely true.

Increased Attention toward Bodily Sensations

Another feature of panic attacks that unfortunately can

heighten your chances of experiencing panic attacks in the future is how ware likely to pay much more attention to your bodily sensations than people who don't have panic attacks do. This phenomenon is known as hypervigilance toward bodily sensations, and it often happens because people are incredibly afraid of having another panic attack that they are always at alert for any bodily sensation that could point to the occurrence of a panic attack. Many people who have panic attacks spend considerable time and concentration scanning their bodies for any bodily sensations in order to catch the first sign of an imminent panic attack. For instance, people with panic attacks may find themselves constantly scanning their bodies to detect any small quickening or their heart rate or breathing. Sometimes, this actually makes a lot of sense as it is a way of establishing a sense of control over something that can seem vastly unpredictable and out of one's control. In addition, who wouldn't want to be able to exercise more control for when panic attacks happen? However the problem with this is that the more attentive you are to these types of bodily sensations, the higher the likelihood that you will pick up these sensations when they're still at very low levels, even far below levels that should concern you. Which also means, that the higher your chances of noticing them, the more likely you'll be to try to avoid them and ultimately, this level of heightened awareness will likely only make you more at risk of having more panic attacks. At this point, the best option is to try learning some skills to broaden your awareness in order to include aspects of your experience more than just the bodily sensations. And as earlier mentioned, dialectical behavior therapy has effective skills that can help you with this.

Noticing And Labeling Sensory Information

Using the dialectical behavior therapy skills of noticing and labeling your experience to focus your attention on your external environment and your sensory information is one of the best techniques to broaden your awareness beyond only bodily sensations. So, instead of restricting your awareness to just bodily sensations, broaden that awareness to include noticing all the information received by your senses. Concentrate on each of your five senses: sight, smell, taste, touch, hearing, and see if you can focus all your attention on your senses one at a time, noticing everything that comes through each particular sensory channel. Do your best not to judge these experiences as either good or bad, just focus on your senses and every sensation you are experiencing in the moment. Then try to begin labeling these experiences, putting the sensory information into words and being as descriptive as you possibly can.

This focus on your external environment will expand your attention beyond just your internal sensations, preventing you from getting too involved in them. Try this the when next you notice you're getting drawn to only your bodily sensations. This chapter contains considerable information on panic attacks and their development. At this point, you've learned a number of different skills that can help you to manage panic attacks effectively. Dedicate some time to practicing all of the skills discussed in this chapter to determine what works best for you. You'll probably discover that some of these skills are more effective for you than others, or that some work only at certain times or in specific situations. The only way to know this is through regular practice of these skills. You must also remember to be patient with both yourself and the skills as trying to reduce avoidance behaviors while increasing contact with feared bodily sensations can be overwhelming. However, the more you practice, the easier it gets, and the more you will see a reduction in your panic attacks. So, begin practicing and start your journey to breaking the hold of panic attacks on your life.

Chapter 7 - Dialectical Behavior Therapy for Individuals with Borderline Personality Disorder and Substance Dependence

Substance use disorders (SUDs) usually accompany borderline personality disorder and lead to complex behavioral problems. This coexistence of SUDs and BPD is second only to how mood disorders and antisocial personality disorder coexist in comorbidity prevalence. Trull and colleagues (2000), found in their extensive review of BPD and SUDs comorbidity data gathered from studies published between 1987 and 1997, that rates of BPD among those seeking substance abuse treatment ranged from 5.2% to 65.1%. Estimates of the prevalence of current SUDs among patients being treated for BPD range from a low of roughly 21% to a high of 67%. Further studies confirm that there's a significant overlap, which is not unexpected, due to the fact that impulsiveness in potentially self-damaging areas like substance abuse is one of the criteria for diagnosing BPD. However, this overlap in criteria doesn't entirely explain the high comorbidity between BPD and SUDs. For instance, Dulit et al. (1990) discovered that 67% of current patients with BPD fit the criteria for SUDs. They saw a drop in incidence to 57%, although still a very significant portion of the population when substance abuse was not used as a criterion of BPD.

It's quite difficult to treat people with BPD and SUDs, given that they have a wider range of problems when compared to people with either SUDs or BPD alone. If the rates of suicide and suicide attempts are already high among people with BPD and substance abusers, then the rates are even higher in those who have both disorders. Even more, substance abusers who have BPD are uniformly more disturbed than substance abusers who don't have a personality disorder. Studies that compare patients who abuse substance with and without personality disorders have reported that patients with personality disorders deal with considerably more behavioral, medical and legal problems, including depression and alcoholism. They are also more deeply involved in substance abuse than patients who don't have personality disorders. A study found the remission of BPD impeded by the presence of a SUD. Some studies of substance-abusing patients that compared those with BPD with people who have other personality disorders found that patients with BPD suffered more severe psychiatric problems than patients who had other personality disorders.

Now how do we justify the high rates of overlap between SUDs and BPD? There are a multitude of interacting factors, including psychological, biological, and sociocultural components that aid the development and maintenance of substance abuse alongside BPD. The high rates of addiction problems suggested in family studies of individuals with BPD shows evidence of a genetic predisposition to the abuse of psychoactive substances in individuals with BPD. Evidence of a link between trait impulsivity and substance abuse also exists. Individuals who abuse substance and have BPD have been found to show higher levels of impulsivity relative to non-substance-abusing people with BPD, which may majorly account for the high rates of concurrent SUDs. Individuals with BPD have an increased risk for addiction problems because of the pervasive emotional dysregulation underlying their disorder. The dependence on psychoactive substances, other problematic behaviors such as cutting, binge eating, hand banging, excessive spending, serves (albeit dysfunctionally) to regulate negative emotions that are out of control. In fact, many individuals with BPD report that their drug usage is how they try to manage their overwhelming emotions, such as sadness, boredom, shame, rage, emptiness, and emotional misery. Biologically, the escape from negative emotions provided by the use of drugs is reinforced by a dopamine spike in a person who has otherwise low levels of dopamine in the mesolimbic area of the midbrain due to extensive drug use over time. Alternatively, substance abuse initially produces pleasure as a result of increases in the dopamine system, but extended use makes it more difficult to experience pleasure sensations because the dopamine system is altered, leading to what Leshner and Koob (1999) refer to as a "changed brain."

Environmental factors also contribute majorly to the development and maintenance of addictive behaviors in people with BPD. Damaging family experiences like abuse, poor communication, conflict, are often observed to depict the histories of individuals with BPD. For a treatment to be effective, it must address the numerous factors that combine to maintain addictive behavior.

What is DBT for Concurrent Substance Abuse and BPD?

Linehan developed the standard dialectical behavior therapy protocol for the treatment of BPD. In using DBT to treat BPD and SUDs, an integrative approach to treatment is adopted to address addiction problems and any other behavioral problems that are specific to individuals with BPD concurrently. DBT for concurrent BPD and SUDs and standard dialectical behavior therapy are the same but for just one difference: It focuses more on addictive behaviors and associated problems. DBT for concurrent BPD is designed to treat multi-disordered individuals with concurrent BPD and substance abuse problems. Similar to the standard DBT treatment, the goals of treatment are:

- To reduce serious behavioral dyscontrol (e.g., substance abuse, suicidal behavior, non-suicidal self-injurious behaviors, excessive and extreme behaviors that interfere with therapy, and other behaviors that significantly interfere with the patients' quality of life),

- And to promote more adaptive, skillful behaviors for functioning in life.

Addictive behaviors, like other impulsive behaviors associated with BPD, are conceptualized as learned behaviors that serve as a means of regulating emotions that may occur in the midst of the chaos of dysregulation. All modes of the treatment protocol, individual therapy, therapist consultation team, skills group, telephone coaching, are delivered just as is obtainable in standard dialectical behavior therapy.

Multiple additional features were added into dialectical behavior therapy for people with both BPD and SUDs so as to make the treatment of substance abuse easier. The treatment modifications are taken from interventions talked about in the substance abuse treatment literature and from clinical experience garnered from applying dialectical behavior therapy to individuals who use substances and who have BPD in several settings. Dialectical behavior therapy for individuals with BPD and SUDs differs from standard dialectical behavior therapy only due to the addition of:

- A conceptual framework for understanding the overlap between BPD and substance abuse,

- A dialectical philosophy to define treatment goals related to addictive behaviors and to address relapse.

- And a modified treatment target hierarchy that includes a focus on substance abuse.

Additionally, several special treatment strategies were incorporated to address the unique needs of patients who have concurrent BPD and SUDs, including a set of attachment strategies directed to facilitate treatment engagement and retention in a population that is notoriously difficult to engage and also specific examples of the dialectical behavior therapy skills customized to the SUDs population.

Dialectical Abstinence

DBT emphasizes the message that to fully enjoy life, abstinence from drug use is the perfect ultimate goal in a Stage 1 treatment. It does this because drug use interferes considerably with living a great life in individuals with severe disorders, including those with BPD and SUDs. However, the sole focus on abstinence usually leaves a real gap when patients fall short, initially described by Marlatt and Gordon (1985) as the AVE "abstinence violation effect." The intense negative emotions that patients generally feel in response to a relapse or mistake can in themselves formulate the very conditions for continued drug use. Especially in individuals with severe disorders in problems of pervasive emotion dysregulation, dealing with the AVE requires teaching and support from the therapist to safely guide them back to abstinence. A dialectical stance on drug use was developed in recognition of the findings that, on one hand, cognitive-behavioral relapse prevention (RP) approaches that are largely dependent on harm reduction principles are useful in reducing the frequency and intensity of drug use after a period of abstinence from drug use, and that, on the other hand, "absolute abstinence" approaches are helpful in lengthening the interval between periods of use. "Dialectical abstinence," which attempts to balance these positions, is a combination of unbending insistence on complete abstinence before any illicit drug abuse and radical acceptance, non-evaluative problem solving, and effective prevention of relapse after any drug use.

Although the end goal in DBT is to keep patients completely free of their drug abuse problems, this goal of abstinence seems unattainable to individuals. The basic idea of the absolute abstinence part of the dialectic involves coaching clients on specific cognitive self-control strategies that allow them to turn their minds completely to abstinence. Patients are specifically coached on anticipation and willfulness, hopelessness, and the weakening of one's commitment to stop drugs that often arises to make treatment complex once a person commits to let go of a dysfunctional habit. Patients are taught that the secret to absolute abstinence is in strongly committing to completely rule out drug use, and it can best be accomplished by being dedicated to abstinence for a certain period of time, no longer than the individual can manage with 100% surety that abstinence will be maintained. The commitment to 100% abstinence may be for any period of time whatsoever, could be 1 day, a whole month, or even just for some hours, it is entirely left to the individual and what they can commit to with 100% certainty. Commitment in this case is mentally "slamming the door shut" for the specified period of time. Once the original commitment period lapses, the individual then recommits to abstinence, and so in this sense, absolute abstinence is achieved by continuously recommitting and "slamming the door shut."

A lifetime of abstinence is achieved one moment or one day at a time - focusing on this one moment, then the next one, and it goes on. The ultimate goal here is to not be able to make half-hearted commitments or deny the reality that you've made one, while also restricting the duration of the commitment to a period that is perceived as achievable by the person's brain.

Other strategies on absolute abstinence cognitive self-control that are used to deceive the brain during this phase include instant "adaptive" denial of desires and options to use during the period of commitment, making an internal deal with oneself that the option to use drugs remains open for the future, practicing radical acceptance of no drug use and the difficulties that come with, and the promise of using drugs when close to death or upon learning of a terminal illness made to oneself. People with SUDs are also taught how to look beyond the moment, plan for danger, and be proactive so as not to resume using. For instance, they are taught to "burn bridges" so they can no longer get drugs, what cues are dangerous for them and how to avoid them. They also learn skills to help them tolerate urges and cravings, with skills for changing their social environment to one more conducive to not using. Knowing which strategy to utilize depends on the most effective one in promoting abstinence and the willingness to maintain it.

Although fully committed to abstinence, dialectical behavior therapy, just like RP understands that all new behaviors requires time and practice to solidify, even those ones associated with abstinence, and that as a result of this, reality slips are likely to happen on the way. The therapist, while maintaining that a commitment to abstinence is important, simultaneously prepares the patient for minimal damage if and when a relapse happens and then helps them return to abstinence as fast as possible. Like RP, a relapse is seen as a problem to solve, not as a failure, and instead emphasize acquiring and strengthening the skill of "failing well." This involves the admission that drug use has happened, and then learning from one's mistakes by carrying out a thorough chain analysis and identifying solutions for future purposes in case a relapse prompting the use of drugs happens again. When coaching patients on how to fail well, there's an emphasis placed on "what if" and "just in case" skills in the event of a crisis. Similar to RP, the therapist and the patient discuss realistic skills and game plans the individual can use if they're in a similar situation in the future. Dialectical behavior therapy, like RP, emphasizes precaution, planning, and preparedness as a way of improving the individual's behavioral control, ultimately leading to better treatment outcomes. You know how a flight crew prepares their passengers onboard for the unlikely event of a water landing or loss of cabin pressure? DBT and RP prepare people to manage inevitable high-risk situation like a potential slip with swift and effective response. Such "drop and roll" emergency techniques include talking to the dialectical behavior therapy therapist, having reminders about their reasons for getting clean, and throwing out drugs so they cannot use them again. Failing well includes analyzing and making amends for the harm caused by using drugs. The focus on correcting the damage caused to oneself and others is similar to making reparations in 12-step programs.

Dialectical behavior therapy incorporates other harm reduction strategies like educating patients about the transmission of HIV/AIDS and hepatitis C, infections transmitted by IV drug use, and other ways of reducing harm if they use drugs. With this, dialectical behavior therapy helps patients to use drugs in safer ways when they do use it, but only on an as-needed basis, while keeping abstinence, the ultimate goal in mind.

Special Treatment Strategies

The specific intervention strategies that were incorporated into dialectical behavior therapy for concurrent BPD and SUDs can be classified into three main categories: (1) a set of attachment strategies designed to handle the increased difficulties with becoming attached to treatment; (2) specific instances for the dialectical behavior therapy skills to deal with urges, cravings with attendant slips, or relapses; and (3) self-management strategies to handle the consequences of living a lifestyle built on a foundation of substance abuse.

Attachment Strategies

While it is important to engage patients in the treatment process, a number of factors can contribute to problems with treatment engagement. Many individuals who abuse substance and with BPD have chaotic lifestyles caused by their pervasive drug use. Some may be unemployed, some may lack adequate housing, living on the street or in crack houses. Some may have resorted to criminal activities to try and support themselves. Some are in dysfunctional and possibly abusive relationships and can't leave because they can't afford it. Drug abuse can disrupt their daily routines such that it's difficult to attend scheduled appointments. Furthermore, denial and lying about one's behavior is usually involved. Individuals tend to downplay their problems, being reluctant to acknowledge their problematic behaviors to themselves or other people which can stem from fear of disclosing their illegal activities or shame about drug use.

Enhancing the patient's motivation and engagement in treatment is a primary treatment task in dialectical behavior therapy. Dialectical behavior therapy sees lack of motivation or disengagement as a problem that needs to be solved instead of an obstacle that needs to be removed before starting treatment. The therapist must be prepared to assume an active role in engaging the patient, and remain steadfast and patient in these efforts.

Dialectical behavior therapy employs several specific attachment strategies to facilitate engagement in treatment of substance-abusing patients with BPD, so as to influence their chances of entering, engaging in, and successfully finishing treatment. The first step the therapist must take is to let the patient know the problem. Openly discuss potential obstructions to treatment engagement, the early warning signs during this orientation phase, and them develop a plan for managing these problems when they arise. Engage supportive family and loved ones early on into treatment to ensure that they are helping to reinforce effective behaviors. During the orientation phase, it is important to create a crisis plan with the patient. This crisis plan should include details of locations they may go if they "get lost" (is in danger of missing four consecutive sessions), and who you may call upon to pull them back into treatment. Therapists should maintain frequent contact with the patient during the first several months of therapy, in order to increase their positive feelings about therapy and the therapeutic relationship. In a situation where the patient "gets lost," the therapist and the team must actively work to reengage him or her, which may include sending cards or a token gift, or even searching for them at home or in their own environment. Based on anecdotal experience, actively pursuing lost patients in their own environment often has a powerful impact, leaving patients pleasantly surprised that anyone even cares enough to pursue them.

When dealing with patients who are hard to engage, the therapists may lack the energy to actively pursue the patient, and so the entire treatment team needs to remain alert to the fact that these patients are likely to burn out even the most skilled therapist, and so the whole team must work actively to support the therapist.

Using Skills to Deal with Urges and Cravings and to Lower Risk of Relapse

The standard dialectical behavior therapy treatment program for BPD has four core skills modules, which are as vital to the treatment of addictive problems as they are for other problems linked with BPD. In patients with SUDs, these core skills are taught as prescribed in the standard arrangement. It was initial thought that it would be necessary to develop new skills, but the standard dialectical behavior therapy are sufficient, with just one exception: the mindfulness skill of Clear Mind, a new skill aimed specifically at addiction.

Clean Mind

The concept of Clear Mind as described above, is essentially helping the patient facilitate the combination of two poles:

- Being clean (clean mind) and

- Being wary of the dangers of addictive thoughts, behaviors and emotions (Addict mind).

To achieve this, the individual therapist and skills trainers highlight moments when the patient may be in "Addict Mind," looking for their next fix and not working toward abstinence, or the "Clean Mind," when the patient is clean, with the belief that the struggle is over. Examples of Addict Mind behavior may include behavior involving trying to score some drugs; stealing; lying; avoiding eye contact; "acting like a corpse"; glamorizing drugs; avoiding doctor; and thinking "I don't have a drug problem."

Instances of Clean Mind behaviors may include thinking it is not dangerous to dress like a drug addict, returning to environments or relationships that fueled your addiction, believing that you can handle the problem alone, stopping medication, thinking "I can use just a little," These signals can help restore your patient back into Clear Mind.

Tailoring the Skills to The Patient

When coaching patients with SUDs on dialectical behavior therapy skills, the therapist must aim the skills directly at drug use behaviors, and have several examples and stories to clearly illustrate each point. A clear demonstration of how the skills can help manage the specific problems and difficulties the patient with SUDs is struggling with is essential. If the therapist has never treated a certain population before, he/she can get examples from other therapists in order to effectively deliver treatment to the population with SUDs.

Mindfulness Skills

Mindfulness skills are extremely useful for treating addiction. Mindful-ness skills can be tailored to the patients particular needs by using the observe and describe skills to help patients acknowledge and face their cravings and urges to use substances. Cravings and urges to use substances are part of the primary precipitants to substance use. There is a lot of anxiety associated with urges and cravings because they are seen as a sign of failure or as a pointer to inevitable relapse. To manage overwhelming anxiety and discomfort, reduce the chances of relapse, the addicted individual may attempt to avoid thoughts and feelings that are related to substance use. Although, this strategy is effective for reducing anxiety in the short term, in the long run, it intensifies urges to use and increases the risk of a relapse.

A technique described by Marlatt (1985) known as "Urge surfing," is a metaphor for the observe and describe skills used to reduce the anxiety linked with urges and thereby lower vulnerability to relapse. The skill includes helping patients disconnect from their urges by applying the observe and describe skills in a nonjudgmental, effective way, which makes the urges more tolerable and reminds the individual that the urge will pass with time. The surfing metaphor includes the strategies essential to successfully cope with urges. The surfer must constantly make subtle adjustments to stay on the crest of the wave without getting "wiped out" by it. If you can stay on top of the wave, the wave will finally die out as it gets near the shore. Denial is a contrary idea to mindfulness, and can be described as surfing with closed eyes and ears while ignoring cognitive, physical and emotional changes. Denying the presence of the waves will not make them go away. Accepting the inevitability of urges and cravings will enable the patient develop a capacity to observe urges with some form detachment while learning to be patient for the wave to crest and pass.

Distress Tolerance Skills

The treatment of substance use requires the use distress tolerance skills. Note that the focus is on using the skills to encourage abstinence and live a life free of substance. An example of such a focus is the use of willing behavior and radical acceptance to "burn bridges" that make it easier to return to substance use. This skill is particularly useful at the initial stage of treating addiction, where the goal is to help the patient curb substance abuse and become stabilized. Once the patient has achieved abstinence, and the focus is now on maintaining stability, the therapist must encourage some exposure to normal cues that may be connected to substance use like attending parties where liquor is served.

"Burning bridges" involves teaching individuals to terminally all options to use drugs as they move from Clean Mind to Clear Mind. It is also important to evaluate how available and accessible psychoactive substances are in the individual's environment. E.g, is the patient selling drugs, or do they work or live with people who use them? The therapist must ask direct questions about the bridges that need to be burned because many patients are unwilling to share this information. Some strategies to reduce their access to substance include cutting off all contact with one's dealer, or intentionally destroying relationships with the dealers so they do not want to provide you with drugs anymore. On the extreme end, Linehan proposed to a patient that she inform her drug dealer that he would be reported to the authorities by her therapist if he didn't refrain from supplying her any more drugs. This is fairly sure way of achieving optimum result.

"Adaptive denial" is a type of pushing away" that changes the characteristic weakness of substance use - self-deception - into an asset. A major challenge substance abusers face is being required to avoid doing something that they intensely desire. Abstinence requires that the patient replace maladaptive behaviors with habits that are less instantly gratifying. Adaptive denial includes pushing away or shutting out possibly accurate but distressing information through self-deception. If for instance, the thought "I can never use drugs again" is usually overwhelming for the patient that it makes them want to give up treatment, avoiding this thought or denying that it even exists, may increase the patient's chances of successfully completing the treatment. Note that patients may get confused by this approach because it's a contradiction of other skills in dialectical behavior therapy focused on reducing avoidance and suppression of thoughts. This poses yet another dialectic in the treatment process, where therapists and patients can judge when denial might actually be effective. Some examples of adaptive denial is a marijuana smoker who convinces himself that he wants to relax in a steaming bath so bad, an alcoholic who persuades himself that he just cannot wait for the first taste of a refreshing glass of cranberry juice and soda water, or the cocaine abuser who watches horror movies because he loves the thrill. They're all tricking themselves away from concentrating on the distress of not seeking relief from what they really want, and engaging in skillful self-deception.

Another skill that can help patients manage intense cravings is reviewing "pros and cons." When overwhelmed by powerful urges, substance abusers usually find it difficult to remember the negative consequences they suffered from their drug use, while experiencing the strong euphoria linked with the psychological and physiological aspects of addiction. Therapists can encourage patients to make a written list of the negative effects of substance abuse and the positive effects of abstinence to be used as a useful concrete reminder not to act on their urges.

Emotion Regulation Skills

The emotion regulation skills are central to dialectical behavior therapy treatment with substance-abusing patients because many target behaviors serve to regulate emotions. Many patients relapse to using drugs at the first sign of difficult emotions, so it is important to keep a strong focus on mindfulness of current emotions. "Opposite action" to emotion enables patients keep from suffering a relapse when they start experiencing these difficult emotions. The PLEASE skills are as well important in addressing the problems with physical pain, sleep, malnutrition, and several other vulnerabilities they often develop.

An example is where a patient had strong tooth pain, that she used opiates - heroin and pain medication - to help her tolerate it. A focus on PLEASE skills became essential because the pain became a cue for her use. A visit to see the dentist, the physician, and get regular dental care and nutrition lessened her pain, in turn reducing her drug use.

Self-Management Strategies

More often than not, substance abuse results in a range of problems that affect all areas of a person's life, including health, job, family, finances, interpersonal relationships, time management, leisure activities. However, there's a dramatic variation in the extent to which substance problems dominate their lifestyle: some patients may lead chaotic lifestyles centered on scoring drugs on the street, while some may lead more stable and functional lives, even have a job while actively committed to their drug habit privately. A majority of the programs for substance abuse acknowledge that the rehabilitation of addicted individuals exceeds just helping them give up drug use, it's also important to help them begin building a healthy lifestyle. To do this, it's necessary to evaluate the extent to which a patient's current lifestyle aids or hinders the recovery process. Helping patient have a "normal" life usually requires assisting them in developing self-management skills and structure building to aid the process. Transitioning from a drug-filled lifestyle to a relatively mundane lifestyle can be incredibly difficult.

As an important part of dialectical behavior therapy, increasing self-management includes coaching the patient on how to apply the principles of behavior change to oneself. In dialectical behavior therapy, patients are basically taught to be their own behavior therapists, executing the agreed change strategies when they're not in session just as their therapist does in session. In dialectical behavior therapy, patients are encouraged to note down each time they implement their own effective behavior in order to strengthen that behavior.

Alongside addressing consequences when implementing change principles; it is also important to manage the cues to urges and cravings to use drugs as a great self-management strategy on the journey to building a drug-free lifestyle. For instance, a patient had smoked marijuana every evening over the past several years. And even though, he got rid of all the drugs and drug paraphernalia from his house, he continually had strong urges to smoke every day. An important step was to help him schedule activities every evening to distract himself from the urges. He signed up for boxing classes and started going to the gym after work, so he didn't go home straight. And as long as his cravings were not satisfied by substance use, the link between the cues and substances would decline over time. In this case, it was crucial that the therapist discuss the concept of extinction.

Lifestyle interventions may also include helping patients achieve structure, such as gaining education/employment, securing accommodation, developing healthy relationships, addressing physical health issues and more. Since it may be impossible for the primary therapist to find a solution to all the patient's problems, the therapist may best serve the patient by enlisting the services of an ancillary case manager as a consultant to the therapist or may consult directly with the patient. An example is an opiate-addicted individual who got employment as a health care aide and had resorted to pilfering pain medications from her patients. After discovery, she was then advised to exit her job and seek empty in less risky settings. Unable to decide on an alternative career choice, her therapist referred her to an employment counselor who helped her identify a more suitable job. Dialectical behavior therapy prioritizes coaching the patient on crises management and accessing essential supports. There is an inextricable link between developing self-management skills and a structured environment because they both involve being mindful of and decreasing the factors that contribute to substance use.

Recently, an effort was made to modify dialectical behavior therapy to target the peculiar needs and capacities of individuals who use substances and have BPD. Dialectical behavior therapy for people with BPD and SUDs embodies the important elements of standard dialectical behavior therapy protocol and specific techniques created to manage issues associated with problematic substance use. Similar to other dysfunctional behaviors associated with BPD, dialectical behavior therapy for substance abusers assumes that an individual's substance use serves as a way of regulating negative mood states. As a result, the treatment focuses on developing more effective strategies to regulate emotions to help patients remove problematic substance use. The goals of dialectical behavior therapy for substance abuse involve getting rid of problematic substance use, building structure, reducing other maladaptive behaviors like self-harm behaviors, removing environmental stressors, and improving overall lifestyle.

Dialectical behavior therapy for substance abuse uses a number of new strategies such as a set of attachment strategies, samples of the dialectical behavior therapy skills designed to address urges, modified hierarchy of targets, cravings to use drugs, and the concept of dialectical abstinence.

Dialectical behavior therapy has been effectively used to treat individuals with BPD and different forms of substance use conditions. Studies conducted on dialectical behavior therapy has found it largely effective in reducing substance use and improving adaptive functioning in many disordered substance-using individuals also diagnosed with BPD.

Chapter 8 - Social Anxiety

Many people are dealing with some sort of social anxiety. In fact the most common anxiety condition is the social anxiety disorder (often termed social phobia). Social anxiety is capable of taking many forms. For instance, some people may feel a little shy about themselves. Others might only get to experience anxiety when they speak in front of big crowds or eat especially in public. And yet some might be afraid of some kind of social circumstance. Irrespective, social anxiety can significantly impact the life of an individual. Think of how many times you're in someone else's company during the day. Probably, there are far too many circumstances to count. It would be very difficult to live your life in such a way that you don't come into any kind of contact with other people. A high degree of anxiety about social situations can profoundly disorganize a person's life and cause some serious suffering.

Situations That Can Bring on Social Anxiety

There are several different situations or events, which are regarded as "social." The most prevalent situation which causes social anxiety is the public speaking (Hofmann and Barlow 2002). Certain kinds of circumstances that can contribute to social anxiety include eating or writing in the presence of other people, being assertive, holding a conversation with someone and using a crowded public toilet. The list goes on and on. People with social anxiety will do all of these things while alone, without fear or hesitation. If these activities need to be performed before someone else (or a whole group) then someone with social anxiety is likely to be very nervous and afraid. This anxiety can often be so high that the individual will be terrified. Social anxiety is usually a product of some type of circumstance or behavior in which there is the possibility of being seen and assessed by others.

Now, the form of circumstances that bring on social anxiety can vary hugely from one individual to the other. Some practitioners in mental health have officially stated that all the social anxieties can be grouped into one of three distinct categories: generalized, non-generalized, and circumscribed. Some people are nervous about only one kind of social situation, like that of public speaking. If they are nor experiencing anxiety in other situations , social anxiety is known to be circumscribed to one kind of situation. In non-generated social anxiety, a person could be nervous in a number of social situations but may feel relaxed in one or more social situations (for instance, talking with another person informally). An individual has anxiety in social situations irrespective of the type of social situation in general social anxiety. The exercise below will help you recognize the kinds of social circumstances that trigger your anxiety.

What Drives Social Anxiety?

Researchers are still researching all the various causes of social anxiety, but one thing is very clear: concern that other people are going to evaluate you seem to be at the fundamental of social anxiety. Most people with social anxiety now worry that others will negatively judge them in social settings. Explicitly, people with social anxiety almost always worry about something they do or say causing others to negate them. And who at least wouldn't be a little nervous about this prospect? Negative evaluation is not something that a lot of people anticipate. Indeed, the association between future negative evaluation and anxiety was so profound that at one time researchers assumed that the fear of negative evaluation was as a matter of fact at the core of the social anxiety. Lately, however, researchers have also started to wonder about the value of positive evaluations too.

There is evidence to think that people with social anxiety will fear a positive evaluation as well as a negative evaluation. This does not seem to make any sense on the surface level. When other people see us in a positive light, it does feel good, right? Okay, maybe not always. Being positively evaluated can make people feel like the bar was raised and that they will have to meet higher expectations in the future. When they assume that such higher expectations cannot be met, either because they think their successful performance was just a flash in the pan, or because they think they can't do any better, they are most likely going to experience anxiety. Getting positive evaluation can as well make people feel like they are now at the forefront, which implies that others will be even more likely to see and judge them.

Consequences of Fearing Evaluation

Being fearful of being judged by other people and the social anxiety you feel as a consequence can have a huge effect on your life. Such concerns will interfere with your performance in some circumstances, your capability to establish close relations with others and your self-esteem, which we will discuss in detail later. The great news is that a range of dialectical behavior therapy skills can help alleviate many of the negative impacts of fearing evaluations. Next, we characterize several prevalent impacts of fearing evaluation and the particular dialectical behavior therapy skills that can help you overcome those side effects. If you encounter other side effects in social environments, see chapters that are explicitly dedicated to these symptoms; the dialectical behavior therapy skills in these chapters are useful to resolve these extra symptoms of social anxiety.

Self-Focused Attention

A lot of people experiencing social anxiety feel that others have high expectations of their conduct and that they cannot meet these expectations. As a consequence, when they are in a social environment, they often concentrate almost all of their attention on their own performance and behavior to ensure they do as much as they can. This really makes perfect sense in some ways. If you want to do better in a situation, paying close attention to what you are doing and actually putting your focus on the way you conduct yourself can be beneficial. The concern is that this degree of self-focused attention will have an adverse effect, particularly if you have anxiety disorder. Picture it this way: since people dealing with social anxiety frequently find themselves in social environments believing that they will never fulfill their audience expectations, they always experience a lot of signs of anxiety, like blushing, sweating, heart rate and trembling. Now, experiencing such signs is not an issue in itself; everyone often gets anxious and some probably don't really know it most of the time. However, when you concentrate all of your consciousness on yourself and into the way you act, these kinds of signs are bound to catch your focus and validate your assumption that you are not fulfilling your audience's expectations. It raises your anxiety, as you may imagine, by leading to a vicious cycle of negative evaluation of your own results and increasing anxiety.

If you are battling social anxiety, you probably understand the disadvantage of putting so much focus on yourself and how hard it can be to break that cycle once you get tangled up in that loop. That is where most of the dialectical behavior therapy skill sets will benefit you.

Redirecting Your Attention Outward

One way that dialectical behavior therapy skills can aid and abet you to escape the vicious cycle of self-focused attention and rising anxiety is by stopping the cycle from forming. And the right approach to do this is to divert your attention to the outside environment. If you experience a high degree of anxiety because of your thoughts about other people, your mind is likely to be focused towards these very signs of anxiety, and your concentration on anything else probably would be very difficult. The dialectical behavior therapy mindfulness skills of observing and characterizing your experience will allow you concentrate your attention on your external environment. Instead of focusing too much on your own behavioral patterns and anxiety symptoms, use these skills to assist yourself get in touch with all the things happening around you. Pay attention to all the aspects of your external world with an emphasis on little information which you sometimes overlook. After that, see if you can give a description of your environment in as much information as possible. What do you see before you? What shapes, texture and colors are you looking at? What sensations or textures can you feel against your skin? Concentrate your efforts into giving details of your environment as accurately as possible.

 If you are overwhelmed by your internal experiences or you find out that you've already shifted focus by paying attention to your anxiety symptoms, making use of the DBT skill of focusing attention on one thing at a time help you shift focus on your external environment once again. Place all your attention on nothing but the world around you, and throwing yourself into characterizing and noticing your external environment and center your mind on that. If your anxiety symptoms distract you, be aware of it, and then slowly return your mind to what you see outside yourself and your body. Do it as many times as you have to, and refocusing your attention over and over again.

Noticing Your Internal Experiences Without Judgment

Dialectical behavior therapy mindfulness skills can help to mitigate the detrimental effects of self-centered thinking in addition to helping you concentrate your thinking on something other than yourself and your inner experience. In particular, you can utilize the dialectical behavior therapy skill to identify your experience without judgment and interrupt the self-directed treatment loop leading you to even more anxiety. Admittedly, while concentrating all of your attention on your inner experiences and anxiety symptoms will often only add to your anxiety, that doesn't have to be the situation. Rather, the explanation as to why this type of self-directed attention almost always comes back to bite is because too many people conclude or judge their anxiety symptoms. You don't have to feel worse when you realize that your heart is pounding or that your hands are trembling. It doesn't need to create issues for you. The issue is that a lot of people get to judge their symptoms of anxiety. Rather than just recognizing their shortness of breath, they pass judgment on themselves and assume that this is a sign of shortcoming or failure. Rather than just observing a racing heart, they evaluate it as deleterious or potentially disastrous. These evaluations, which most often go together with observations of symptoms of anxiety, create issues. Only recognizing the signs does not harm you, in and of itself.

So make sure to take a non-evaluative stance when you become aware of your anxiety and the bodily sensations that follow it. Permit yourself to be aware of these experiences without you evaluating or judging them. Instead of judging it as negative, poor, sad or incorrect, concentrate on only recognizing and labeling every part of your experience as it is. Bear in mind that anxiety and all of its feelings are just a natural part of being alive and something that every individual experiences. Analyzing your inner perceptions in this manner will help you identify with the fact that your anxiety symptoms are not detrimental in and of themselves. And this will go a long way towards helping you stop the habit of self-centered attention resulting in increased anxiety, leading to even more self-centered attention, and so forth.

Attention to Potential Signs of Negative Evaluation in Your Environment

Now, as much as mastering how to divert your awareness to your external environment is likely going to help some of the issues that go along with concentrating all your awareness on yourself and your inner experiences. You see, researches have shown that people with social anxiety are much more likely to observe and focus exclusively on things in their environments that are frightening or indicate that their feelings of anxiety may be valid.

Let's say, for example, that you are speaking openly to a massive audience. If you have social anxiety, the one person in the crowd who frowns will usually catch your attention, even though there are other people who are laughing and sending you valuable feedback. Furthermore, once your attention is focused on that person, it will be difficult to turn your focus away from the face of the person. Moreover, while the person can be frowning at a number of different things, once your attention is primarily focused in this frown, you will see it as an indication that you are not doing quite well, thereby leading to more anxiety and further shifting your awareness to anything damaging in your environment. Therefore it is important not only to concentrate your attention on your external world, but to extend your knowledge to include all aspects of your world. If you find yourself concentrating on only one individual or aspect of your life, practice on trying to expand your focus to be able to gather all information around you. This will allow you to relate your performance to a more balanced evaluation.

This is another moment when it may be useful to note the experience without judgment or evaluation. Instead of assessing what you find in your environment, simply take notice and define it critically, discouraging any evaluations to take place. Now, you can find that these evaluations tend to pop up from time to time, particularly as you begin practicing this skill. This is normal and should be expected. If this happens, just take notice of this evaluation or judgment and refocus your attention to the observation and description of things around you. The aim is not to eliminate evaluations and judgments entirely, but to adjust how you react to these forms of thoughts such that you do not get entangled in them.

When your eyes are fully open and you observe all facets of your environment without evaluation, it can also help immensely to really throw yourself into, or indulge yourself in, whatever thing you are doing at the moment. If you're speaking to a crowd, put your entire mind and body into the presentation, make it the most significant activity in your world at that moment. As a matter of fact, you can consistently do that, regardless of whatever it is you are doing, and it will almost always benefit you.

Avoidance of Social Situations

One big way that social anxiety can intervene with a person's life is by resulting in avoidance. If you experience extreme anxiety in social environments, you may want to reduce your anxiety by staying away from these types of situations. But as already described, avoiding all social situations is virtually impossible, and trying to do so will greatly restrict your life. Attempting to avoid social situations leading to anxiety can interfere with maintaining strong relationships or building new relationships. This would also impact the types of work you will do, because too many work require speaking in the presence of other people or being judged by others. Ultimately, attempting to avoid social interactions might literally restrict your daily life activities, since too many involves being around other people. While the urge to escape circumstances that cause anxiety is understood in all these respects, acting on this urge probably won't work on the longer term and will likely just contribute to your discomfort. So a large part of overcoming social anxiety is breaking down the avoidance it creates, and the DBT ability to work against the fear will help with that.

Approaching Feared Social Situations

As I already stated, avoiding situations that you fear would only intensify your fear if these things aren't necessarily dangerous or harmful. If the social environments that people with social anxiety fear were actually very dangerous or life-threatening, I would educate you on the skills you can use to stop them, in the same way we would advise children not to follow strangers. However, with social anxiety, individuals learned to fear all forms of social situations not necessarily harmful. So as they avoid these circumstances, their anxiety persists and can escalate. So, just as we discussed under panic attacks and PTSD symptoms, the way to overcome this fear and prevent social anxiety from harming your life is to address the circumstances that you have always stayed away from.

In order to start applying this skill to social anxiety, the following exercise can be used to identify all social situations that have been avoided in your life. In the first column, write down these conditions. Recall that the number of individuals present in these situations can differ from one to two people to massive crowds.

Next, consider taking some quick, proactive measures to get to grips with these situations. What can you do to place yourself in these circumstances? Ponder on all the things you can do to get in contact with these circumstances and take small measures to combat your anxiety. For example, if you're scared to eat before others, you may be able to start by chewing gum or snacking peanuts before your best friend as you go down the main sidewalk. You don't have to begin with a five-course dinner in the presence of your new date. All you have to do is break down these things one step at a time. Try writing down the steps you're going to take.

As I have said throughout this book, the recognition of the steps you should take to end the sequence of avoidance in anxiety disorder is a major first step in resolving the anxiety in your life. It can actually be incredibly frightening to think about handling these issues, and it is a vital step on the path to recovery to take the time to consider the things you can do to get in touch with these circumstances. The next step is to get through this list, to do one thing at a time in order to tackle these circumstances and overcome your fear.

Using anxiety management skills. Now we know that it's actually better to tackle the situations that frighten you the most. Even if you understand the concepts behind the skills to work against your fear and logically understand that avoiding these circumstances would only intensify your anxiety, it can still be unbelievably challenging to tackle them. And if you do start to take action to tackle these conditions, you will probably experience a great deal of anxiety. Therefore, it may be helpful to incorporate the skill of acting contradictory to your fearfulness with other DBT skills that can help you overcome anxiety, as you begin to tackle your dreaded social situations.

There's a pretty simple but one of the most useful skills for tolerating anxiety: breathing. As surprising as it is, many people don't know how to breathe properly, making a lot of people breathe in ways that can actually increase their anxiety. So, a basic way of managing anxiety is simply learning how to breathe correctly: using your diaphragm to breathe. The diaphragm is the muscle between your lungs and your stomach.

How to know if you're breathing properly? Breathe in and out slowly and as you breathe, observe the parts of your body that move in and out or up and down. If you are breathing correctly, your belly should stretch outwards when you inhale and go back in when you exhale. If your belly expands and contracts as you breathe, you are breathing with your diaphragm, but if your shoulders move up and down when you're breathing, you are probably not breathing properly, and may be at risk for more anxiety.

Breathing with your diaphragm will help you breathe deeper, which translates into slower breathing. Taking deep, slow breaths is how your body naturally combats anxiety. Even more, breathing out slowly can lower your heart rate when you are anxious. Hence, deep breathing is one of the most basic techniques for tolerating anxiety.

Not Getting Your Needs Met in Social Situations

It's practically impossible to avoid most social situations, which means you have to find other ways to deal with the intense anxiety that arise from unavoidable social interactions. A common way of doing this is by trying to limit the chances of negative evaluation by avoiding any kind of conflict. For instance, some people with social anxiety avoid standing out in social situations in such ways as speaking softly, avoiding eye contact, or not expressing their needs. And, for a person whose goal is to avoid conflict or negative evaluation, these kinds of behaviors are understandable. These behaviors can influence social interactions in some ways, such as making it unlikely that people will notice you. Also, the chances are reduced that you'll say something upsetting or offensive to other people - which could lead to negative evaluation. These behaviors can also plant the notion that you are incapable of managing social interactions, which can reduce your self-respect and self-esteem. Additionally, behaviors such as this can also lower the chances of positive evaluation by other people, which, as earlier discussed, can be damaging for someone with social anxiety.

However, a major disadvantage of this strategy is that your needs will probably never be met in these interactions, which may lead to you feeling unimportant and as if you are not being taken seriously. Some good news, though, is that there are some really useful DBT skills that help people get their needs met while also maintaining their self-respect and good relationships with others.

This is a really important point to note: assertiveness and asking for your needs does not mean that you should ho around upsetting people or sacrificing those relationships in your life. Many people make this common mistake. The DBT interpersonal effectiveness skills focus on helping you balance getting your needs met, while also keeping your self-respect and maintaining strong relationships.

Getting What You Want Out Of Your Interactions

How then does this set of skills work? The first step you should take is to know what you want to achieve from the interaction. What are your goals? Do you want to get something specific from other people it for you want to decline a request? Figure out what you want.

Secondly, have a script that helps you state your needs and ask for what you want. Start by laying out the situation as clearly as possible, while making sure to describe it objectively. After that, tell the person your feelings about the situation with statements starting with "I feel" and "I think." This is a chance to explain your opinions about the situation and perspectives. Next, lay out your needs what you want and what you want them to do for you as specifically as possible.

Finally, explain to them how giving you what you need will be advantageous to them too. This step is not usually found in basic assertiveness training, but it is incredibly important with the goal of explaining to the other person upfront that they stand to benefit from doing what you're asking of them and that it is a win-win situation.

At this point, you've probably realized that getting your needs met is actually not as simple as merely asking for your want. Sometimes, those people may not be capable or even willing to meet your needs, regardless of how skillfully you ask! Following these discoveries, is one more step that you need to take to prepare yourself for this interaction. This last step requires you to think about the compromises you are willing to offer if the person cannot or is unwilling to give you what you are asking for. It's important to think about this ahead of time as it can be difficult to think in the thick of the moment, trying to consider all of the consequences of several options when you are already having an interaction and experiencing anxiety. You should commit to doing this and identify beforehand, the compromises that are acceptable or not to you, so as to make the interaction go as smoothly as possible in event of any problems. Try using this exercise to prepare for an upcoming interaction.

Steps for Getting Your Needs Met in Interpersonal Interactions

1. Simplify what you want from the interactions. Ask yourself questions like: What do I want to achieve from this interaction? What are my goals for this interaction?

2. Now design a script stating your needs and explaining what you want.

3. Practice this script as many times as you need to and until you are absolutely comfortable with it. Stand in front of a mirror, or with a close friend or loved one and practice the script. Bring your focus to nonverbal cues along with the words you are saying.

4. After having prepared, approach the other person and proceed to ask for what you want.

Remember that just like anything else, this skill become easier with practice. Also note that the more you practice asking for your needs from other people, the more comfortable you will get and the more likely it is that your needs will be met. Also, you may want to pair this skill with some of the skills that help with tolerating anxiety that have been taught earlier, such as deep breathing and PMR.

You should also learn to balance your needs with those of your relationships. Similar to how the DBT mindfulness skills earlier described specifies not only what to do but how to, the DBT interpersonal effectiveness skills also place a major focus on the approach to saying the things you want to say and the most useful way of delivering your request.

Here are some pointers to remember when asking for what you want or need in a relationship.

- Always focus on the purpose of the interaction; don't get distracted by other issues. It is pretty easy to start bringing up other relationship issues that you are upset about when you're talking about your concerns about someone's behavior. Avoid falling into that trap as much as you can. Rather, keep the purpose of that particular interaction at the forefront of your mind and stick to it. Doing this will probably be exceedingly more effective than talking about other issues or previous issues.

- Express yourself in a clear, calm, and confident tone. Keep your voice at a normal volume and at all costs, refrain from raising your voice or speaking too softly. Also concentrate on keeping a relaxed posture and facial expression, as this will help you feel more relaxed. Ensure you maintain eye contact when speaking.

- Never disrespect the person you are speaking to. Try to listen to their response and validate their feelings or perspective on the issue. Speak directly and genuinely in the interaction. Respect the validity of their opinion even if you disagree with them.

- Describe your position honestly, and do not lie or make excuses. Remain true to your position and don't doubt the validity of your request.

Negotiating relationships is difficult and can be a stressful experience, even for people who don't have social anxiety. And being assertive in relationships can be an understandably daunting task, however expressing your needs and asserting yourself will only strengthen your relationships and make it more fulfilling. Like all the other skills we've discussed, the more you practice this skill, the easier and more comfortable you will get with them. So, consider what you want from any upcoming interactions and follow these steps to help you get your needs met. Remember that you deserve this.

This chapter contains a lot of information on social anxiety and various skills that may be useful in overcoming it. Understand that being comfortable and confident in social situations is a process that requires time and practice. Sometimes, you may be really pleased with skillfully you handled a social situation and other times, you won't think you handled it as well. That is understandable but unfortunately, you can't control how other people respond. Which means that times will be when you will get negative feedback from people no matter how skillfully you handled it or regardless of whether deserve it or not.

Just know that the most important thing is to do the best you can in social situations and understand that you are human. So, remember to be kind and patient and compassionate with yourself as you practice these skills, and you will discover that you are getting better on the journey of overcoming your social anxiety.

Conclusion

Dialectical behavioral treatment is a form of psychotherapy or talk therapy using a cognitive-behavioral approach. The dialectical behavioral treatment emphasizes treatment psychosocial elements. The idea behind the theory is that certain people are likely to respond more emotionally and out of the ordinary to certain emotional circumstances, especially those found in interpersonal, family and friendly relationships. Dialectical behavioral treatment theory suggests that certain people's arousal levels in such circumstances can rise much faster than an average person's own, reach a higher level of emotional arousal, and take significant time to get back to baseline arousal levels.

People who are often dealing with borderline personality disorder experience intense changes in mood, see the universe in black-and-white colors, and often seem to leap from crisis to crisis. Since few people understand these reactions - mostly their own relatives and a childhood that highlighted invalidation - they have no methods to cope with these unforeseen, intense emotional surges. Dialectical behavioral treatment is a teaching skills approach that can help in this challenge.

Dialectical behavioral treatment is based on three main

theoretical frameworks. These theoretical frameworks are behavioral science biosocial paradigm for chronic mental health situations, dialectic philosophy and mindfulness practice.

Biosocial theory seeks to clarify how borderline-personality disorders evolve. The theory suggests certain people are born predisposed to emotional weakness. Environments lacking stable structure and stability can exacerbate a person's negative emotional reactions. They can as well greatly affect interaction patterns that are devastating. These patterns can seriously damage relationships across all situations. They often lead to suicidal thoughts and/or borderline personality diagnosis.

Dialectical behavior therapy derives mindfulness practices from Zen Buddhism to utilize here-and-now mind presence. This can help people evaluate circumstances critically and respectfully in therapy. Mindfulness training or preparation helps individuals to analyze their existing understanding, identify facts and concentrate on one mission at a time.

Dialectics are used to aid and abet the person in treatment and the therapist. They draw from both sides of a problem. The therapists use dialectics to help individuals embrace things they don't like. They often use dialectics to provide inspiration and encouragement to tackle these parts transition.

Dialectical behavior therapy's standard form is made up of

individual counseling, telephone counseling, skills training group, and a therapist consultation team. Those in standard dialectical behavior therapy put in an appearance at therapy and skills training group every week. Groups are put in place to help therapists improve the coping skills of clients by means of homework and group training. These tasks allow people to practice skills learned in everyday life. In addition, phone counseling or coaching is a vitally important component of dialectical behavior therapy. It enables people in the treatment to be able to reach out to their therapist for help or support when a challenging circumstance arises between sessions.

The problems facing many dialectical behavior therapy participants can be complicated and serious. As a result of this, consultation team is also deemed necessary for dialectical behavior therapy providers. The team comprises individual therapists and group leaders. It can provide therapists working on complicated issues with inspiration, support and therapy.

Dialectical behavior therapy is the perfect treatment method for individuals with Borderline Personality Disorder (BPD) and also for those with other mental health conditions. Dialectical behavior therapy is an excellent tool to teach you how to keep your emotions under control. It is also useful for people with addictions and need skills to control their cravings, or who are traumatized and don't feel as if they are unable to cope with the trauma. However, dialectical behavior therapy is not an alternative intervention for trauma, because it does not include any care and treatment.